THE OLD FEDERAL ROAD

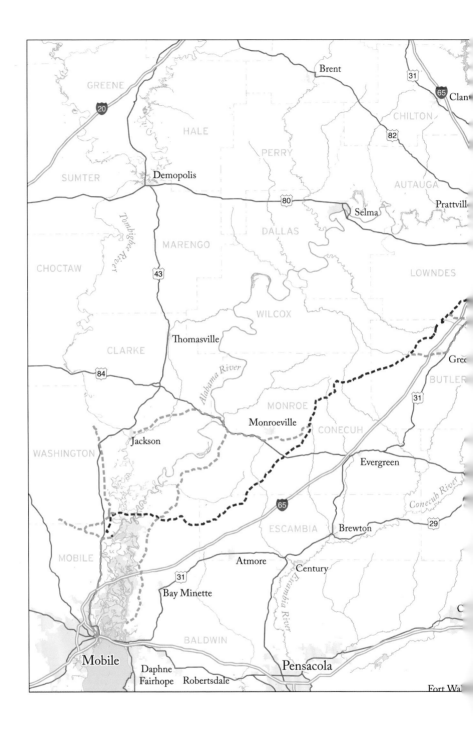

Alabama
THE FORGE OF HISTORY

A SERIES OF ILLUSTRATED GUIDES

An Illustrated Guide

THE OLD FEDERAL ROAD IN ALABAMA

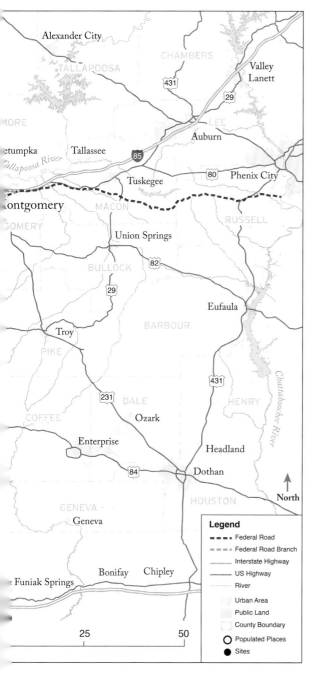

Legend
- ▬ ▬ ▬ Federal Road
- ▬ ▬ ▬ Federal Road Branch
- —— Interstate Highway
- —— US Highway
- —— River
- Urban Area
- Public Land
- County Boundary
- ○ Populated Places
- ● Sites

North

Kathryn H. Braund, Gregory A. Waselkov, and Raven M. Christopher

The University of Alabama Press / Tuscaloosa

The University of Alabama Press
Tuscaloosa, Alabama 35487-0380
uapress.ua.edu

Frontispiece. Overview of the Federal Road in Alabama.
Map produced by Brad Sanders.

Copyright © 2019 by the University of Alabama Press
All rights reserved.

Inquiries about reproducing material from this work
should be addressed to the University of Alabama Press.

Typefaces: Minion Pro, Myriad Pro, and Engravers MT

Manufactured in China

Front cover image: James Weakley's 1834 survey plat of Township 16 North,
Range 30 East, showing the Old Federal Road labeled as "United States Mail
Road"; courtesy of the Bureau of Land Management, General Land Office
Back cover image: Old Federal Road Historic Marker; courtesy of Kathryn H. Braund
Cover design: Todd Lape / Lape Designs

Library of Congress Cataloging-in-Publication Data

Names: Braund, Kathryn E. Holland, 1955– author. | Waselkov,
Gregory A., author. | Christopher, Raven M., author.
Title: The Old Federal Road in Alabama : an illustrated guide /
Kathryn H. Braund, Gregory A. Waselkov, and Raven M. Christopher.
Description: Tuscaloosa : The University of Alabama Press, [2019] |
Includes bibliographical references and index.
Identifiers: LCCN 2018044470| ISBN 9780817359300 (pbk.) | ISBN 9780817392598 (e book)
Subjects: LCSH: Federal Road (Ala. and Ga.)—History. | Federal Road
(Ala. and Ga.)—Tours. | Roads—Alabama—History. | Alabama—History.
Classification: LCC F326 .B83 2019 | DDC 976.1—dc23
LC record available at https://lccn.loc.gov/2018044470

CONTENTS

I. THE OLD FEDERAL ROAD: A HISTORY

II. TOURING THE OLD FEDERAL ROAD IN ALABAMA

ILLUSTRATIONS

MAPS

ACKNOWLEDGMENTS

This book grew out of two related projects. The first, spearheaded by Gregory A. Waselkov and Raven M. Christopher, was an archaeological survey of the Old Federal Road in Alabama, a Transportation Enhancement grant project administered by the Alabama Department of Transportation.[1] That work led to related archaeological research in conjunction with the Pintlala Historical Association, with excavations at the site of Manack's Store.[2] The second project, one of a series of rural development initiatives related to tourism and the Old Federal Road funded by a mini-grant from the Alabama Cooperative Extension System, permitted development of this guidebook.

The authors particularly thank Dr. Richard Guthrie, whose vision of rural development resulted in myriad projects to enhance our understanding and appreciation of the Old Federal Road. Several people tested our driving directions and made suggestions that improved them. We are indebted to Shari Williams, Beth DeBusk, and T. R. Henderson for taking up the test drive challenge. Special thanks to Brad Sanders for producing the maps for the driving tours based on early drafts by Sarah Mattics and Raven M. Christopher.

We also thank the following repositories for the use of images and maps from their collections, reproduced here with their permission: Alabama Department of Archives and History; Auburn University Library, Special Collections; Bartram Trail Conference; Beinecke Rare Book and Manuscript Library, Yale University; Brent McWilliams Family; Center for Archaeological Studies, University of South Alabama; Archives Nationales d'Outre-Mer, Aix; Greenville County Museum of Art, Greenville, South Carolina; Telamon Cuyler Collection, Hargrett Library, University of Georgia, Athens; David Rumsey Map Collection; Doy Leale McCall Rare Book and Manuscript Library, University of South Alabama; General Land Office, Bureau of Land Management, US Department of the Interior, Washington, DC; Historic New

Orleans Collection; Jule Collins Smith Museum of Fine Art, Auburn University; Library of Congress; Lilly Library, Indiana University, Bloomington, Indiana; Mark Dauber; Mississippi Department of Archives and History; Mobile History Museum, Mobile, Alabama; *Montgomery Advertiser*; Mount Vernon History Trail; National Archives, Silver Spring, Maryland; National Museum of American History, Smithsonian Institution, Washington, DC; National Portrait Gallery, London; North Carolina Department of Archives and History; Skillman Library, Lafayette College State Historical Society of Missouri, Columbia; and the Vischer Family.

We are especially indebted to Mary Ann Neeley. Her vision and passion for historic preservation and early Alabama history stirred interest in the Old Federal Road, stimulating public interest and enthusiasm that resulted in funding for study and discussion of the Old Federal Road through myriad programs and projects. We dedicate this book to her memory.

I

THE OLD FEDERAL ROAD

A HISTORY

INTRODUCTION
Opening the Federal Road

Two horses picked their way between innumerable stumps freshly cut days before by ax-wielding soldiers. Enveloped by a seemingly boundless forest, the riders measured their progress by the numerals chopped crudely into one blazed pine trunk, then another, and another: I . . . II . . . III . . . the miles from Mims's Landing on the Alabama River . . . CX . . . CXI . . . CXII . . . counting down their passage ever deeper into the Creek Indian Nation. Lorenzo Dow, already widely known for his eccentric, exhilarating style of preaching, and his wife Peggy were going home after years in the southwestern territories carrying the word of Primitive Methodism to the remotest settlements of the young United States.

Now and then they met small bands of travelers heading south, the first wave of immigrant families to travel this new Federal Road bound for the rich lands along the Tensaw delta and the lower Tombigbee River, and more distant Natchez and New Orleans. One large family, Peggy noted, had something "like a tent" to cover them at night from the cold rains of early December. The Dows lacked even that scant comfort, camping in the open at the end of each long day. Before bedding down they cut river cane as forage for their horses and gathered wood for their fire, praying that the flickering light would fend off wolves and allay Peggy's fears of human predators in this "lonely desert." For in fact there were only a handful of residents along this new Federal Road, half a dozen Creek families willing to offer simple meals and a night's shelter to travelers. Lorenzo and Peggy permitted themselves no more than a few hours of sleep each night, wrapped in blankets under the starry heavens, before they would press onward. Like others on the road in 1811, the Dows knew they must cover ground rapidly, thirty to forty miles a day, if they were to traverse this "long and tedious wilderness" on the small bag of coffee and hard biscuits they carried for provisions.

Peggy Dow. From *The dealings of God, man, and the devil; as exemplified in the life, experience, and travels of Lorenzo Dow, in a period of over half a century: together with his polemic and miscellaneous writings, complete. To which is added: The vicissitudes of life, by Peggy Dow ... With an introductory essay by the Rev. John Dowling*, 2 vols. in 1 (New York: Cornish, Lamport, 1850). Courtesy of the Auburn University Library, Special Collections.

After eleven days of constant hardship, Peggy suffered a fall from her horse "and hurt myself considerably." Still she persevered and rode into Milledgeville, "the metropolis of *Georgia*," to recuperate for a week with friends. She wrote in her journal, "I was as much fatigued and worn out by travelling as ever I was in my life. I thought sometimes that I never should stand it, to get through the wilderness, but Providence gave me strength." On December 16, 1811, a few days after reaching Milledgeville, the Dows experienced the first of the New Madrid earthquakes, the greatest tremors to strike the eastern United States in historic times. "It was truly an awful scene," Peggy wrote, "to feel the house shaking under you . . . and the trees as it were *dancing* on the hills." One could scarcely imagine a more apt harbinger of the changes that would transform the people and land the Dows had just traversed on the Federal Road.[1]

THE GREAT EARTHQUAKE AT NEW MADRID

The Great Earthquake at New Madrid, 1811–1812, from Henry Howe, *Historical Collections of the Great West*, vol. 2, p. 237 (Cincinnati, OH: E. Morgan, 1851). Courtesy of the State Historical Society of Missouri, Columbia.

The road was open at last. The Dows were among the first to travel this controversial and barely tolerable path through the wilderness. Seven years had passed since an initial reconnaissance in 1804 by an East Coast surveyor who twice lost his way. Four years earlier, contractors inexperienced with southern forests had bungled an expensive effort to clear ancient Indian paths for postal riders. Only now, fourteen months since Creek Indian warriors ignominiously disarmed a work party of US soldiers widening the mail path, did American diplomats, surveyors, and engineers coordinate efforts and complete the task of building a road across four hundred miles of the Creek Nation. By the winter of 1811, despite obstacles and setbacks, the Federal Road from Milledgeville, Georgia, to Fort Stoddert in Mississippi Territory had become a reality.

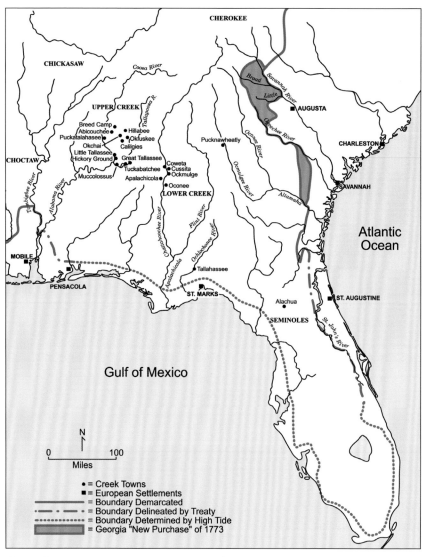

The Creek Country, ca. 1773. Based on maps produced by cartographers working for the British Superintendent of Indian Affairs. Courtesy of Center for Archaeological Studies, University of South Alabama.

ONE

EARLY PATHS AND ROADS

The foundation of the Federal Road was laid by Indian feet. For countless generations, Indian travelers, hunters, and warriors charted and maintained paths that penetrated forests to connect Indian towns with one another, linking them to hunting and fishing resources and to the South's great river systems, the other half of the region's communications network. Sensibly, early Indian paths—not much wider than their human creators—literally followed the path of least resistance, most commonly traversing ridges that divided river systems. High dry paths avoided swamps, canebrakes, and streams, inevitably descending to the most hospitable river and stream crossings as destinations dictated. With the emergence of European settlements along the coast, particularly British Charleston and Savannah, Spanish Pensacola, and French Mobile, Indian footpaths took on new importance, ultimately developing into horse paths that supported a leading economic engine of the southern colonies, the deerskin trade.

These trading paths between European and Indian towns, over which hundreds of packhorses traveled annually, were not very wide and were kept clear by the trampling of hoofs. In 1773, the British cartographer Bernard Romans recommended a new road be cut from Pensacola to the Creek Nation and noted the ease with which it could be done. After marking the route by blazing trees, Romans thought that "the passage of about 100 packhorses (a number not much exceeding what the traders now bring to Pensacola at one time)" would be sufficient to establish the new road.[1] Routine clearing of downed trees and debris was undertaken by travelers, who also had to swim deep rivers and construct their own rafts to ferry merchandise.

For native peoples the roads that connected them to outsiders carried symbolic meanings. Indian speakers invoked the "beloved" or "white" path to denote peaceful relations and alliance, while Indian diplomats worked strenuously to keep all paths between natives and colonizing Europeans metaphorically "straight" and "free of bushes and impediments." Indeed, the major trading artery linking the Creek Indians to Anglo-American settlements was known as the "old beloved path."[2]

The most famous colonist to travel along the main Creek trading path that would become the Federal Road was William Bartram, a peripatetic Philadelphia botanist whose tour of the South lasted nearly four years and carried him an estimated 2,400 miles through eight modern states. He entered the Creek Nation in July 1775, crossed the Chattahoochee River at Yuchi town, then proceeded to Apalachicola, deemed "the mother town or capital" of the Creek confederacy,[3] close by the better-known town of Coweta, near modern-day Phenix City, Alabama. Bartram was traveling on the main trading path that linked the Lower and Upper towns of the Creek Nation, heading toward Mobile. After a brief stop, the pack train with which he traveled took three days to reach the Upper Creek town of Tallassee, on the Tallapoosa River, crossing "a vast level plain country of expansive savannas, groves, Cane swamps and open Pine forests, watered by innumerable rivulets and brooks."[4] The travelers then followed "the great trading path for West Florida"[5] and Mobile, which lay 175 miles to the southwest. After exploring the Mobile-Tensaw delta and visiting the Mississippi River, Bartram retraced his summer trek in late November in the company of another caravan of deerskin traders driving thirty or so horses. Although he appreciated safety in numbers and the assistance of experienced hands who knew the countryside, their pace of travel proved wearing. In his well-known book, *Travels*, Bartram described the "mad manner" in which traders pushed their horses: "they start all at once, the horses having ranged themselves in regular Indian file, the veteran in the van, and the younger in the rear; then the chief drives with the crack of his whip, and a whoop or shriek, which rings through the forests and plains, speaks in Indian, commanding them to proceed, which is repeated by all the company, when we start at once, keeping up a brisk and constant trot, which is incessantly urged and continued as long as the miserable creatures are able to move forward." No doubt the pace was necessary, for, between the British settlements in the Mobile-Tensaw delta and the Creek towns at the head of the Alabama River, the land was devoid of permanent human habitations. Travelers had to be self-reliant as they faced the elements alone. In addition to sheltering

William Bartram, wax portrait by Donna Weaver, based on an original portrait by Charles Willson Peale. Courtesy of the Bartram Trail Conference.

from storms by standing under trees, sleeping in the open, foraging for food, and keeping watch for robbers or unfriendly Indians, travelers faced a greater risk—their inability to acquire new horses on the trail. When Bartram's horse faltered, he feared he would "be left alone to perish in the wilderness."[6]

While most early paths followed the high ridges between drainages, which eased travel immeasurably and surely must account in part for the long popularity of the route followed by the Federal Road, there were places where streams and swamps simply could not be avoided. Crossing a creek or river, particularly during floods, could be dangerous. Near Indian towns, locals helped canoe travelers and their goods across rivers, but on the trail travelers were left to their own ingenuity, as Bartram found when he and a companion had to cross a large creek swollen with winter rains. There were myriad hazards, including snags, raging currents, snakes, and alligators. In inhabited areas, dugout canoes might be available for use at well-frequented crossing

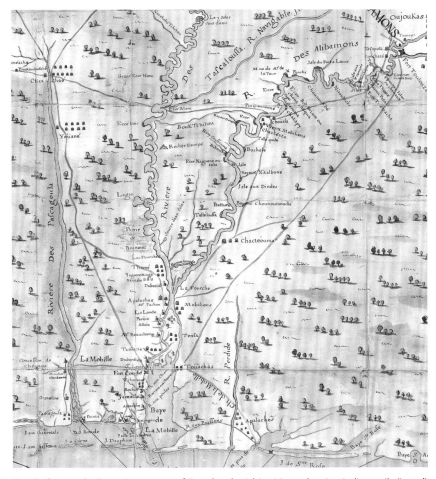

Detail of Baron de Crenay's 1733 map of French colonial *Louisiane*, showing Indian trails (in red) in the area that would later become southwestern Alabama. The easternmost trail running from Fort Toulouse to Mobile Bay, called by the French "chemin des Alibamons" for the Alabama Indians residing near their fort, corresponds generally with the path that became the southern portion of the Federal Road. Courtesy of the Archives Nationales d'Outre-Mer, Aix.

points, but usually those hoping to traverse rivers and streams were forced to swim or construct rafts. At one large flooding stream, Bartram watched in amazement as his Indian companion quickly constructed a raft from logs, dry cane, and vines to ferry their goods across. Horses, forced to swim the churning waters, faced the same hazards as human swimmers and were sometimes snared by snags or simply overcome by swift currents. Once a river was successfully crossed, travelers found additional challenges, as did Bartram and his companion, in the form of a deep gulley with banks fifteen to twenty feet high. Their solution was "a sapling felled across it, which is called a raccoon bridge, and over this my Indian friend would trip as quick and light as that quadruped, with one hundred weight of leather on his back, when I was scarcely able to shuffle myself along over it astride."[7]

The path William Bartram followed from the Upper Creek towns to Mobile in the 1770s, which would become a major segment of the Federal Road, had in former years seen little traffic. Indeed, the end of the Seven Years' War marked a sharp break with traditional patterns of trade, exchange, and travel throughout the Creek Nation. Prior to 1763, most overland traffic in this portion of the South had followed an east–west course, reflecting commercial ties between the Creeks and British South Carolina and Georgia. Contact with Spanish Pensacola was sporadic, while diplomatic relations and trade with the French centered on Fort Toulouse, connected to Mobile by river. After the ouster of French and Spanish colonial administrations from the northeastern Gulf Coast and the establishment of British traders in Mobile and Pensacola, formerly minor paths to the Gulf Coast suddenly became major routes for trade with the interior. But the coming of the American Revolution ended this burgeoning economic development.

Like their colonist neighbors, the Creeks were divided by the war. Some towns, notably among the Upper Creeks, gravitated toward the British loyalists, while others inclined to neutrality. Indeed, as one Lower Creek headmen related, the Creeks "had like to have made a War among" themselves. Although divided over the best course for their own interests, the Creeks avoided civil war. But the end of the revolution brought dramatic changes to the Creek country, including sizeable land cessions to Georgia and a shattering of the old deerskin-based economy.[8]

After the American Revolution, with Florida back in Spanish hands, the "old beloved path" that led from Augusta and Charleston into the Creek Nation fell into disuse as Americans took more interest in establishing farms than continuing to trade with Indians. Moreover, business connections that had long linked major trading houses in Georgia and South Carolina to Britain were irrevocably broken as aging loyalist traders retired or were driven from the former colonies. Many of them relocated beyond the boundaries of the young United States, and one firm in particular—Panton, Leslie, and Company, operating under Spanish auspices—carried on the southeastern deerskin trade from Pensacola (with the Creeks) and Mobile (with the Choctaws and Chickasaws).

Benjamin Hawkins and the Creek Indians, circa 1805, unidentified artist. Courtesy of the Greenville County Museum of Art, Greenville, South Carolina.

Dramatic accompanying shifts in communication and transportation patterns left fewer avenues for mutually beneficial interactions between the Creek Nation and the new states to their east and north. A rush of American settlement on the Georgia frontier and in what is today Tennessee strained Creek-American relations, which had never recovered from Creek assistance to the British during the revolution. Only in 1790, with the Treaty of New York, did Creeks and Americans end a prolonged period of border warfare. Along with normalized relations came America's new "civilization policy" and Benjamin Hawkins, a meddlesome federal agent, as well as a host of new economic endeavors designed to replace the near moribund deerskin trade. As Creeks sought to restrict access to and through their territory, to protect their remaining lands from outright seizure and their traditional culture from the corrosive effects of growing American influence, Americans increasingly sought open access. By the early nineteenth century, US officials were demanding road and water routes through Creek lands as a national right. As Hawkins pointedly told the Creek chiefs in 1811, "if the people of the seventeen white fires choose to travel by land or water thro' the country of the red fire, they have a right to do it."[9]

The Creeks, among the most proficient farmers in North America, did not raise crops for commercial markets. Hawkins and the American civilization plan sought to change that. But paths suitable for horse traffic were ill-suited for wagon transport of crops—and, indeed, there were few nearby markets for such goods. Thus, the "civilization policy," flawed in concept and hampered by reality, instead aimed to make Creeks self-sufficient by producing homespun cloth, shift their economy from deer hunting to livestock raising, and "reform" Creek government in order to facilitate American demands for land and roads. For their part, most Creeks had already adopted new economic endeavors, primarily stock keeping. This had a profound impact on Creek settlement patterns, as families moved away from densely packed towns and built homes in the countryside for the benefit of plentiful forage for their cattle. Some Creeks came to own increasing numbers of enslaved African Americans, whom they employed to tend livestock. Slaves also served as status symbols in Creek society, as wealth was measured in chattel property. Thus, along with the traditional trade in hides and other produce, many Creeks sold cattle and traded horses and slaves in the expanding exchange economy, especially the one developing around the Mobile-Tensaw delta at the junction of Spanish, American, and Creek territories. By the time of the Louisiana Purchase in 1803, Creeks were finding new ways to engage with American and colonial commercial exchange networks that supplied the guns, cloth, and other manufactured goods now considered necessities by the Creek people.

The Louisiana Purchase doubled the size of the United States with the acquisition from France of 827,000 square miles of land, or, rather, a transfer of a European imperial claim to native-held lands. The prospect of unsettled lands encouraged westward expansion by American citizens and brought demands for improved overland transportation routes to the new territory, particularly to the prize of the purchase: New Orleans. A sudden necessity to defend that port city, as well as American settlements at Natchez and other parts of Mississippi Territory, also called for better communication links. In 1803, the best route from Washington, DC, to New Orleans took postal riders and travelers through the Appalachian Mountains to Nashville, and then down the Natchez Trace—a distance of more than 1,500 miles.[10] So "destitute of water and articles of subsistence" was the harsh terrain of Cherokee country that mail carriers hauled their own food, horse fodder, and water "carried in goat skins." And that isolated route was "infested with robbers." Faced with such formidable obstacles to timely communication with the newly acquired territory, the Committee on Post Offices and Post Roads unanimously recommended

Detail from Abraham Bradley Jr.'s 1796 *A Map of the United States*, showing an absence of post roads in the southwest during the earliest years of the United States. Courtesy Library of Congress.

Congress consider a new route by which "the mail may be conveyed with greater facility and dispatch."[11] The most direct alternative to supplant the Nashville–Natchez Trace route would slice through the Creek Nation.

Benjamin Hawkins, among others, offered advice and assistance in promoting and scouting this new route. He was certainly qualified to provide expert testimony on the subject. During his many tours of the Creek Nation, Hawkins kept a travel journal, a "viatory," in which he jotted down brief descriptions of geographical features encountered on Indian paths. Several entries in his viatory describe paths that would become the basis of the new federal

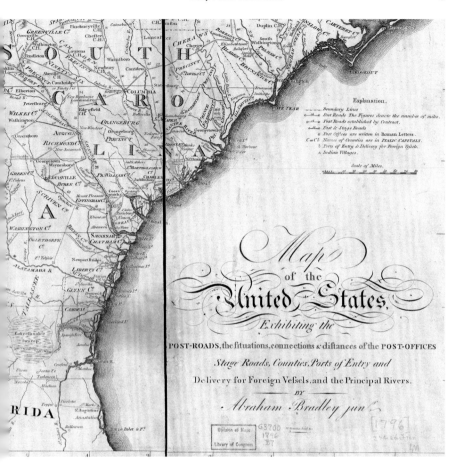

postal road. For instance, over the course of five days in June 1799, Hawkins rode north from John Randon's plantation, east of the Mobile-Tensaw delta, to Sehoy Weatherford's trading house among the Alabama towns of the Upper Creeks. Along the way he kept track of his predominant compass bearing and noted his riding time between topographic features, particularly the streams and paths he crossed. His journey's notes begin as follows:

N. 1.20 + c. l. 10/. Hollow Creek
1. + c. l. 15/ Turkey Creek

Thomas Foster, who edited Hawkins's viatory for publication, interpreted his
method of notation. Following Foster's lead, these entries can be decoded as
follows:

> Bearing North. At one hour twenty minutes, crossed Hollow [now Holley]
> Creek, 10 feet wide, flowing left.
> At one hour farther on, crossed Turkey Creek, 15 feet wide, flowing left.

This sort of log is clearly not equivalent to a measured survey, since Hawkins's travel bearings are generalizations and correlating travel time to distance traveled would depend on terrain, weather, and other factors. Hawkins's
rate of travel on this path averaged about three miles per hour over about fifty
hours of riding. Despite its lack of precision, Hawkins's viatory is the earliest
detailed account of the path that would become the southern portion of the
Federal Road, and it provides many insights into the nature of the Indian path
before major alterations by American road builders.

As in Bartram's day, no one lived along the path, although Hawkins did
intersect eight other paths, which hints at the complexity of the trail network
that once crisscrossed this uninhabited region. He mentioned by name the
Wolf Trail, referring to a major path to Pensacola that he passed "three minutes" below Burnt Corn Spring, and the "trading road," also known as the
Tuckabatchee path. Of the thirty-four creeks and branches he encountered
on the path, just three—Limestone, Pintlala, and Catoma—were wide enough
to pose challenges to travelers. In fact, Hawkins found many streams and
branches dry during his June traverse. Although only passable in 1799 by foot
or on horseback, Hawkins considered the Alabama–Mobile path and others
documented in his viatory to be prime candidates for development into roads.
And that, we can safely assume, was Hawkins's motivation to create his viatory in the first place. As the ranking US official in the Creek Nation, all of his
actions were driven by his certainty that the burgeoning population of the
eastern states would expand westward. What better basis for roads through a
"wilderness" than a network of pathways refined by native travelers over the
centuries?[12]

Hawkins's advice no doubt helped shape the 1803 proposal for a mail route
from Washington, DC, through the Creek Nation to New Orleans, a route then
estimated to be five hundred miles shorter than the existing route through
Nashville and Natchez. Hawkins must have provided the details found in a
House of Representatives resolution of December 1803 that called for "a post

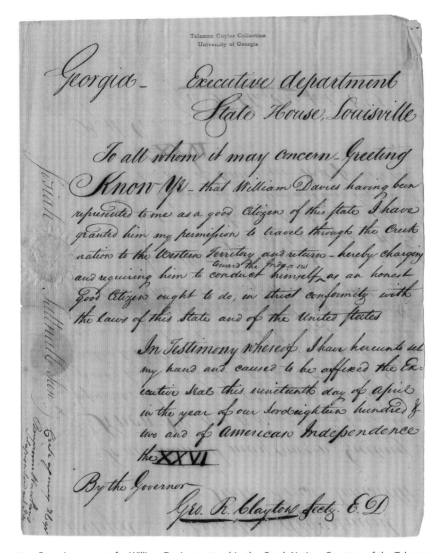

1802 Georgia passport for William Davies to travel in the Creek Nation. Courtesy of the Telamon Cuyler Collection, Hargrett Library, University of Georgia, Athens.

road . . . to pass through or near the Tuckaubatchee settlement, to the Tombigbee settlement, in the Mississippi territory, and from thence to New Orleans; and also from the said Tombigbee settlement to Natchez."[13]

The House resolution cited as a further advantage the proposed route's passage "almost the whole way through a country inhabited either by citizens of the United States, or friendly Indians." In truth, there was little support among the Creeks for American transit across their lands—the 1790 treaty with the United States specifically restricted travel through the Creek Nation—and their continued friendliness could not be assumed. Secretary of War Henry Dearborn understood this impediment to a new road and in February 1804 instructed Hawkins to raise the issue with Creek leaders.[14]

As those negotiations began, President Jefferson persuaded Isaac Briggs, recently appointed surveyor general of the Mississippi Territory, to return from Washington, DC, to his post near Natchez via the Indian paths Hawkins had traveled a few years earlier. He was to report to President Jefferson on the true length of this potential mail route based on sound scientific measurements of important way points. Briggs, a skilled surveyor and astronomer, was a colleague of the eminent Andrew Ellicott, who had surveyed the boundary line between the United States and Spanish Florida a few years earlier. But, unlike Ellicott, Briggs proved no frontiersman. His journey across the Creek Nation nearly killed him. Nevertheless, his reports to Jefferson and his field notes reveal much about the difficulties of travel and surveying in that era.

Briggs and his assistant, Thomas Robertson, entered the Creek Nation from Georgia on October 6, 1804. They set off without a guide and immediately became lost, "wandering many miles astray in the wilderness" until coming upon the store of an Indian trader. In retrospect, Briggs wrote, "I had an idea that I could pass through this country without a path or a guide, but when I mentioned it on the frontiers of Georgia it was scouted [that is, scorned] and laughed at." Severe storms delayed the team for two days, during which "the ear could scarcely distinguish an interval between the sound of one falling tree and that of another." After failing, despite their best efforts, to procure a guide for the sixty miles to Hawkins's Creek Agency, the hapless pair set out alone and again became lost. Briggs estimated they wandered at least 112 miles, "frequently climbing over precipices, wading through swamps, and crossing deep and difficult water courses, many miles without a path, our horses greatly incommoded and fatigued by sensitive briers and other vines. Our provisions were soon wet and spoiled and we were in danger of starving, not having seen a human face except each other's for more than four days. On the 15th we arrived at Col. Hawkins's on Flint River."[15]

After recuperating for five days, they set out with a packhorse, provisions, and, finally, a guide (all provided by Hawkins) and reached "Point Comfort" a week later. Point Comfort was Briggs's name for one of Hawkins's agency establishments south of Tuckabatchee operated by his assistant and

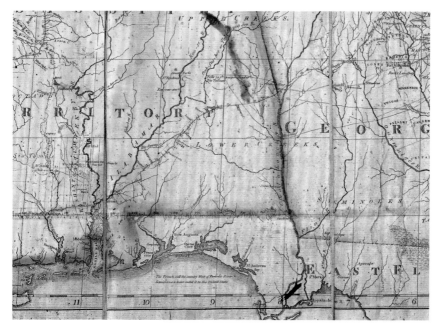

Detail from Abraham Bradley Jr.'s 1812 *A Map of the United States*, showing the path across the Creek Nation derived from Bloomfield's 1807–11 notes. Courtesy David Rumsey Historical Map Collection.

interpreter, Alexander Cornells (Oche Haujo), the headman or *mico* of Tuckabatchee. The journey there, which covered just 120 miles, was, wrote Briggs, "most laborious both to our horses and ourselves." A heavy rain had swollen the rivers and streams. As a result, the surveyors' "horses swam the Chattahoochee River from shore to shore, and six creeks between that and this place. In short we arrived here much fatigued." The surveyors rested a week at Point Comfort and discussed their plans with Cornells. When asked about the efficacy of a road through the nation, Briggs claimed that Cornells "expressed a full concurrence with me in the opinion that facility of intercourse which such a road would occasion would be highly beneficial to the red people as well as to the white." If true, Cornells was certainly one of the few Creeks to hold that opinion. Continuing their journey on November 3, by the ninth they reached "the house of Nathaniel Christmas, on the west side of Tombigbee River about two miles above its confluence with Alibama [that is, the head of the Mobile River]." Of this last stretch, Briggs wrote: "From Point Comfort to Mobile river is (excepting a few swamps of no very great extent, which must be causewayed) a fine, high, level, sandy ridge." The pair delayed the last leg of

A transit and equal altitude instrument made by Henry Voigt of Philadelphia and used by Isaac Briggs in 1804 to establish a prime meridian for the United States running through Washington, DC. Briggs took the instrument with him through the Creek Nation to Natchez, Mississippi Territory. Courtesy of the National Museum of American History, Smithsonian Institution, Washington, DC.

their adventure when news reached them from New Orleans of an outbreak of yellow fever that had taken the life of Briggs's younger brother.[16]

Considering the hardships Briggs and Robertson endured, their surveying accomplishments offered a meager return. Their route map is no longer extant, but Abraham Bradley incorporated a sketch of the route into his 1812 map of post roads in the United States based on an 1811 survey. These early maps were crude affairs, barely a step beyond the sort of map Hawkins could have made from his time and bearing log. Their major goal, at President Jefferson's insistence, had been to obtain accurate latitude and longitude calculations at a handful of points along the route, so a precise distance between Washington, DC, and New Orleans could be calculated. Using the only instrument available to him, a surveyor's pocket sextant, Briggs calculated reasonable approximations of latitude and longitude for three points along the paths that would become the Federal Road—just three points!

Briggs explained the difficulties of his task in a letter to Jefferson. Determining longitude at any given point along his path proved his greatest challenge. During a nighttime observation, two major stars had to be visible "at the same instant," free of cloud cover, as he calculated their distances above the horizon and their distance apart. Since the natural horizon was always obscured in hilly forested terrain, Briggs relied on an "artificial horizon, consisting of a reflecting fluid surface," which was too often roiled by even the slightest breeze. And due to the imprecision of his poor-quality instrument, he had to take many observations to obtain a reasonably accurate average. "I have frequently sat nearly a whole night, exposed to a heavy dew, and in the day time for hours to a burning sun, in both cases without the protection of my hat, anxiously watching for a momentary interval of a little clear sky and calm atmosphere; and have been often at last disappointed. Considering these and many other exposures to heat, wet, cold, bad provisions, &c. it is a matter of wonder and of gratitude to a merciful God that my health was not sooner destroyed."[17]

Briggs began his measurements at "the President's House" (the White House) in Washington, DC, which he determined to be situated at 38° 53' 00" N Latitude. For his survey purposes he patriotically established the longitude there as 0° 00' 00" (corresponding to 77° 02' 12" W Longitude, by modern convention). His calculations for Creek Nation landmarks yielded the following results:

> Indian Agency: *32° 39' 00" N Latitude, 07° 25' 11" W Longitude*
> Point Comfort: *32° 23' 19" N Latitude, 09° 08' 38" W Longitude*
> Mouth of Alabama: *31° 06' 57" N Latitude, 11° 04' 48" W Longitude*

The Flint River Agency location, Hawkins's gravesite today, is well known and can serve as a check for us on Briggs's calculations. The last two points fall along the Federal Road in Alabama. Point Comfort's precise location, unfortunately, is uncertain. Briggs offered ambiguous descriptions of the place in his letters to Jefferson, describing it as "About 2 miles south of Tallapoosa river, and about 5 miles S.W. of the southeasternmost bend of the river," and later as the "southeasternmost projection of Tallapoosa River," or "2 miles south of Tallapoosa River, and about 5 miles S.S.W. of the Town of Tookaubatchee."[18] A few years later the Federal Road ran about six miles south of the big bend of the Tallapoosa; Point Comfort might have been located near Polecat Springs, which is six miles south-southwest of the big bend and about four miles from the river. As for the "Mouth of Alabama," Briggs could have meant the Cut-off, where the Federal Road later crossed the Mobile-Tensaw delta, but we assume he meant the actual mouth of the river, about four miles northeast of Fort Stoddert.[19]

If we convert Briggs's latitudes to modern form, his calculations fall quite close to modern values, with a consistent southerly bias of generally less than 1 minute of latitude or about a mile. Surveyors in his day, however, had much greater difficulty determining longitude. Lacking better equipment, and in particular an accurate chronometer, surveyors like Briggs had to determine their east–west position by calculating Greenwich Mean Time through astronomical observations. Attempting this famously difficult feat with a substandard instrument introduced substantial error into Briggs's longitude calculations, which were consistently too far west by 11 to 21 minutes (and as many miles). In the end, Briggs's principal accomplishment was his demonstration that a mail route across the Creek Nation would indeed shave off about five hundred miles in comparison with the trans–Appalachian/Natchez Trace route then in use. Jefferson and others seem to have discounted the difficulties Briggs encountered on his journey. Other Americans would soon find his obstacles to travel across the Creek Nation all too real, the principal one being the Creeks themselves.[20]

TWO

BUILDING A FEDERAL ROAD

Benjamin Hawkins and other US officials recognized Indian objections to roads through their lands, and they worked assiduously to lay the ground-work for an expanded transportation network across the Mississippi Territory by negotiating new treaties with all of the southern Indian nations in 1805. Prominent among the treaty clauses were rights to establish "horse paths" across several of those nations for use by US post riders, military troops, and other Americans. For example, Article 2 of the 1805 Treaty with the Creek Indians reads as follows:

> It is hereby stipulated and agreed, on the part of the Creek nation that the gov-ernment of the United States shall forever hereafter have a right to a horse path, through the Creek country, from the Ocmulgee to the Mobile, in such direction as shall, by the President of the United States, be considered most convenient, and to clear out the same, and lay logs over the creeks: And the citizens of said States, shall at all times have a right to pass peaceably on said path, under such regula-tion and restrictions, as the government of the United States shall from time to time direct; and the Creek chiefs will have boats kept at the several rivers for the conveyance of men and horses, and houses of entertainment established at suit-able places on said path for the accommodation of travellers; and the respective ferriages and prices of entertainment for men and horses, shall be regulated by the present agent, Col. Hawkins, or by his successor in office, or as is usual among white people.[1]

Hawkins and the other American negotiators gained the assent of the Indian nations for these very unpopular road clauses in the treaties by sweetening the deal for the leaders who signed for their people. By stipulating the chiefs as responsible for building and operating causeways, ferries, and "houses of entertainment" along the horse paths, chiefs were sure to benefit handsomely from tolls, lodging fares, and tavern tabs. So great were expected profits that at least one Creek leader tried to alter the route in places to bring coveted traffic closer to his residence.

While treaty language clearly anticipated eventual use of the "horse paths" by immigrants, for US officials, extending an efficient mail service into the southwestern territories was the most pressing need. Dispatches sent between Washington, DC, and New Orleans, whether by ship or overland by the long route through Tennessee and down the Natchez Trace, routinely took a month or more in transit. The US postal service of this era depended on private contractors for mail delivery. Therefore, in August 1806, Postmaster General Gideon Granger contracted with Joseph Wheaton to establish a postal route between Athens, Georgia, and Fort Stoddert, Mississippi Territory, generally coinciding with the path followed for years by travelers through the Creek Nation. Wheaton's contract required him to open a four-foot-wide bridle path or horse road, to span all swampy places with "causeways," to fell trees as footbridges across narrow streams, and to encourage Indians to establish ferries at larger stream and river crossings. By October his postal riders were expected to be picking up the mail "from Coweta [on the Chattahoochee River] every Sunday at 2 A.M. & [to have] delivered it at Fort Stoddert the next Tuesday by 10 P.M. in three days nearly, [and] to have left Fort Stoddert every Wednesday at 2 A.M. and delivered it at Coweta by next Friday at 9 P.M."[2]

Contractor Wheaton soon found these tasks to be more difficult than either he or the postmaster general imagined. Several separate parties of ax men cleared sections of the route in the fall of 1806. At the north end, Wheaton and several of his men became seriously ill with fever and abandoned their clearing project after two weeks, without completing any bridges or causeways. This brief experience in the wilderness seems to have discouraged Wheaton from further personal involvement in the project, and he henceforth hired others to run the postal service. Zachariah McGirth, an American living in the Creek Nation, momentarily agreed before realizing the impossibility of meeting the delivery schedule. Wheaton then recruited another expatriate American, Samuel Bloomfield, to take the subcontract. By mid-1807 an investigation by the Post Office Department concluded the "mail has in no instance been carried in this time required by contract." In fact, because Wheaton had offered his mail carriers so little money to carry the mail through Indian country, "it was not even attempted."³ Eventually Postmaster General Granger came to oppose additional "large expenditures in unsuccessful attempts to force rapid mail service through an immense wilderness filled with streams and marshes where no sustenance or aid can be given to either man or beast."⁴

A regular mail route was finally established through the Creek Nation due to the persistence of Benjamin Hawkins. After Wheaton's ineffectual effort to open a path, Hawkins worked with the US military to make the route passable for horses, hired Creek Indians as post riders, and, most importantly, encouraged the Creeks to establish along the route those "houses of entertainment" called for in the treaty. Because the upper portion of the path passed close by existing native settlements, several prominent Creeks, such as William McIntosh at Coweta, took advantage of the business opportunities created by the new road—just as US treaty negotiators had hoped in 1805—and opened their homes to travelers and post riders. But the lower path toward Fort Stoddert had no permanent settlements. Hawkins, therefore, persuaded two wealthy Creeks to build houses along the path—Samuel Moniac at Pintlala and James Cornells at Burnt Corn Spring—where post riders could rest under shelter and find fresh horses. Moniac's place on the path, in particular, played a pivotal role in the history of the Federal Road and of the Creek Nation.⁵

Samuel Moniac built a "place of entertainment" or "station" (using Hawkins's terms) at a place called Pintlala in 1808 or 1809.⁶ Its actual location was a few miles southwest of the Pintlala Creek crossing and a short distance west of Pinchona or Pinchony Creek. Hawkins thought the primary function of stations along the mail path should be to supply extra horses and fodder, which would enable riders to switch to fresh mounts and keep the mail moving on its way. However, the incremental improvements to the path accomplished on behalf of the Post Office Department made the route increasingly attractive to the US Army and to immigrants, a fact not lost on the Creek Indians. When Samuel Bloomfield, one of Wheaton's former subcontractors, "entered with his waggon and team and commenced and built bridges" in 1810 on the upper path, the Creek National Council voiced a valid objection that the Treaty of 1805 allowed only ferries across streams and logs over creeks, not American-controlled bridges, which would cut into the profits Indians could derive from ferry traffic and toll bridges along the path.⁷

The American military took the next provocative step toward road development in September 1810, when the regional military commander at Fort Stoddert conveyed an order from the secretary of war to Lieutenant John R. N. Luckett to survey and clear the "Indian path East of Alabama [River] to the

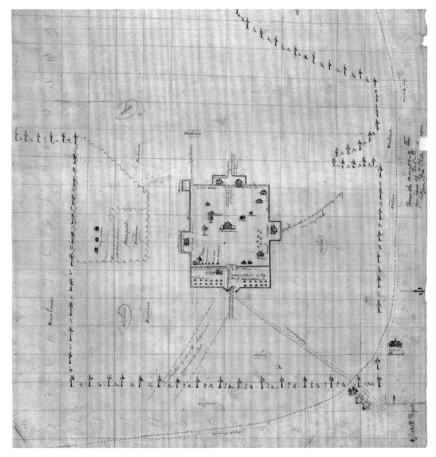

The "Claiborne Map" of Fort Mims, 1813, showing the location of Mims's Ferry on the Alabama River and the Mims house and outbuilding and stockade erected as the Creek War erupted. Courtesy of the Alabama Department of Archives and History.

forks of Coosa and Tallapoosa," purportedly so the government might acquire "a more correct knowledge of the rivers and country than they have hitherto had."[8] This detachment of a dozen or so soldiers from the US Second Infantry Regiment wielded axes to clear the mail path once again, while Lieutenant Luckett used compass and surveyor's chain to produce a bearing and distance survey—what Henry Deleon Southerland Jr. and Jerry Elijah Brown called "the first simple, one-line or center-line survey for road construction in Alabama."[9]

The lieutenant began his survey of the path, not from Fort Stoddert, but from the mouth of Holly Creek at a ferry operated by Samuel Mims, whose

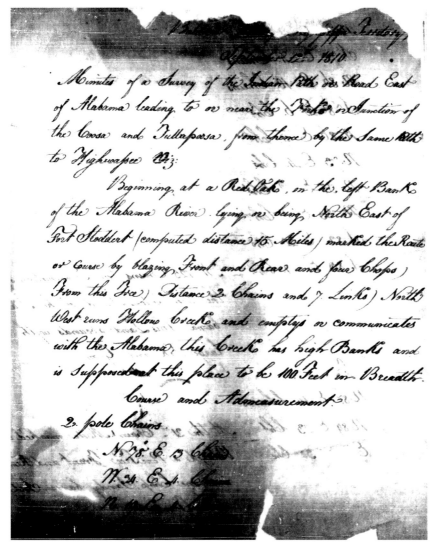

Lieutenant Luckett's survey, journal page of September 12, 1810. Record Group 77, Records of the Office of the Chief of Engineers, Field Survey Records, 1793–1918, #37-4-7. Courtesy of the National Archives, Silver Spring, Maryland.

house stood a mile to the east. Luckett blazed trees with Roman numerals at the mile marks and noted the quality of soils and vegetation along the route as well as the locations and widths of streams and swamps. The need to constantly clear the same path will come as no surprise to anyone familiar with the undergrowth of southern forests, but it also reflects how traffic in 1810 had declined from the levels witnessed by William Bartram at the height of the deerskin trade. Despite at least five years of use as a mail route, Luckett found the track difficult to follow; at one point he followed the wrong path for seventeen miles before discovering his error and backtracking to Mile 10. On October 5, the survey party's twenty-fourth day on the job, near Mile 123 they crossed "a Road [on] the Right from my course leading to Maniac's [sic] a wealthy half Breed." Incidentally, Moniac's house was not directly on Luckett's path because the lieutenant had diverged westward from the Indian path at Mile 107, an innovation not followed by later road developers. Three miles farther, just across the great "Palawla" [Pintlala] swamp, Lieutenant Luckett's survey abruptly stopped.[10]

Although the taciturn lieutenant's journal entries simply end without explanation, contemporary accounts reveal that the Creek Indians halted his survey prematurely. From his vantage point at the Creek Agency in Georgia, Benjamin Hawkins learned on October 8 "that the party is coming on from Fort Stoddert with their compass and chain and the explanations they give not satisfactory to the Indians and that the whole of the upper towns are alarmed and probably will stop the detachment."[11] A news account published in the *Georgia Journal* a few days later reported Luckett's party "arrested near Mannacs, (a half breed) by a party of 300 or more Indians."[12]

In a meeting at Tuckabatchee in late October 1810, Creek leaders told Hawkins and Luckett that "the measuring and marking their country should be stoped for the present." A second survey party led by Captain Edmund P. Gaines, mapping another route through the western part of the Creek Nation, was disarmed at about the same time, and both detachments were escorted back to Fort Stoddert. Even so, American civilians continued to move westward along the path through the Creek Nation.[13] By the following October Hawkins was adamant the horse path should be widened, as the president of the United States had ordered. He told the Creek National Council, "the period has now arrived when the white people must have roads to market and for traveling wherever they choose to go through the United States. The people of Tennessee must have a road to Mobile [the one Captain Gaines had been surveying], and the post paths must become a road for travellers and both of these roads will be used by the troops of the United States in marching from post to post as the public good may require." He further held the chiefs responsible for ensuring that their young men did not commit crimes against any of these travelers. Hawkins harangued the chiefs of the Creek Nation for days before they agreed, reluctantly reconciling to the "new evils they were likely to experience" due to the road and the travelers it was sure to bring. Units of the US Third Infantry Regiment were allowed to expand the horse path into a true road, widening and bridging and causewaying at a rate of about five miles per day. Two detachments, one working from the east, the other from the west, met near Moniac's place on November 30, 1811, at which date the Federal Road finally became a reality. The ancient Indian path had been transformed.[14]

All of the Americans tasked with opening a horse path for postal riders—Briggs, Wheaton, Granger, Luckett—considered this land a wilderness, unimproved and untamed by civilization, just so many unimproved acres of unexploited agricultural potential, a view shared by many European and American travelers on the Federal Road. From their perspective, road building would begin the process of civilizing the landscape. On the other hand, the Creek Indians occupied a landscape given meaning by their experiences and those of their ancestors over hundreds of generations, a rich history recorded in thousands of place names and constantly recalled as they traversed the region's maze of paths for hunting and trade and a multitude of other reasons. This vital landscape was no wilderness, no vacant unimproved land to be given up to covetous neighbors. Labeling Indian lands as wilderness was a constant refrain of American expansion. After centuries of interaction with colonial and American officials, the Creeks knew there was more to this road than a "horse path" for mail riders.

From this time forward, civilian traffic on the Federal Road increased markedly. Hawkins reported over 3,700 immigrants with 120 wagons, 80 carts, 30 "chairs," and 3 "four-wheel Carriages" moving west on the road through the Creek Nation between October 1811 and March 1812.[15] The itinerant Methodist minister Lorenzo Dow and his wife Peggy rode east that winter, and her journal entries give us a rare description of travel on the road in its earliest days.

> We were now in the bounds of the *Creek* nation: we were still without any
> company.—This day we struck the *road* that had been cut out by the order of the
> *President*, from the state of Georgia, to Fort *Stoddard*. This made it more pleasant
> for travelling, and then we frequently met people removing from the States to the
> *Tombigby*, and other parts of the Mississippi territory.
>
> We travelled betwixt thirty and forty miles that day, and came to a creek,
> called *Murder* creek: it got this name in consequence of a man having been
> murdered there. This circumstance made it appear very gloomy to me. But we

STATE OF GEORGIA.

By his Excellency *David B Mitchell*

Governor and Commander in Chief of the Army

and Navy of this State and of the Militia thereof.

To all to whom these presents shall come, or whom the same

may concern. . . . . Greeting:

KNOW YE, that the bearers hereof *Mssᵈ Isaac Jackson & Lawrence Meed from Anna County North Carolina have*

my permission to travel through the *Creek* Nation *they* taking special care to conduct *themselves* peaceably towards the Indians, and agreeably to the laws of the United States.

In testimony whereof, I have hereunto set my hand and caused the Executive Seal of the State to be affixed thereto.

Done at the State-House in MILLEDGEVILLE, the ——— 6 day of *May* in the year of our Lord one thousand eight hundred and *Eleven* of the Independence of the United States of America the thirty-*fifth*

BY THE GOVERNOR.

James Bonpeau

Passport issued by Georgia Governor David B. Mitchell, 1811. Courtesy of the Mississippi Department of Archives and History.

made the necessary preparations for the night, and lay down to rest: although I was so much afraid, I got so weary at times, that I could not help *sleeping*. About twelve o'clock it began to rain so fast, that it was like to put out our fire, and we were under the necessity of getting our horses and starting, as we had nothing to screen us from the rain. The road having been newly cut out, the fresh marked trees served for a *guide*—there was a moon, but it was shut in by clouds. However, we travelled on ten or twelve miles and it ceased raining: I was very wet and cold, and felt the need of a fire, more perhaps than I had ever done in my life before! . . .

We came across a family who were moving to the Mississippi—they had a number of small children; and although they had something to cover them like a tent, yet they suffered considerably from the rain the night before: and to add to that, the woman told me they had left an aged father at a man's house by the name of *Manack*, one or two days before, and that she expected he was dead perhaps by that time. They were as black almost as the *natives*, and the woman seemed very much disturbed at their situation. I felt pity for her—I thought her burthen was really heavier than mine. We kept on, and about the middle of the day we got to the house where the poor man had been left with his wife, son, and daughter. A few hours before we got there, he had closed his eyes in death—they had lain him out, and expected to bury him that evening; but they could not get any thing to make a *coffin* of, only split stuff to make a kind of box, and so put him in the ground! . . .

We stayed but a short time and continued on our journey. There we got a sup- ply of bread, such as it was; and there we met with three men that were travelling our road, the first company that we had found since we had left the Mississippi, being now not more than one-third of the way through the *Creek nation*.[16]

The Dows reached Milledgeville, Georgia, two weeks later and Peggy noted in her journal, "while we were here the *earthquakes* began, which alarmed the people very much." These were the first of the New Madrid earthquakes that began on December 16, 1811, which helps us date Peggy Dow's visit to Moni- ac's house on the Federal Road. Her account also suggests how basic were the amenities available to travelers at this station—"bread, such as it was"; no sawn planks for a coffin.[17]

Traveling the Federal Road in these early days entailed a certain amount of risk. There were always chances of accident, drowning, snakebite, illness, and the rarer possibility of injury inflicted by others. In 1805 a post rider named Webb, while "walking after his horse" along the path "in an open plain with a cluster of plumb trees only near him . . . was fired on from behind the plumb trees" about four miles from Catoma, not far from Pintlala. "He saw no one; as soon as he was wounded he fell down and fainted. . . . His saddle bags and bag of corn were left untouched. . . . The mails were gone and the staples of the saddle drawn to which they were attached."[18] Webb recovered, but thieves often targeted mail riders, and seemingly random attacks on others occurred now and then as well.

The widened and improved horse path for these mail riders drew an ever-expanding stream of American immigrants through the Creek Nation. With each traveler, Creek opposition to the Federal Road steadily increased. Tension between the United States and Britain aggravated the situation, as more official traffic headed for the Gulf Coast and war between the two seemed certain. Many Indian peoples came to believe this was the time for decisive action against the Americans, and against their own leaders who signed treaties allowing road construction and otherwise abetted American interference in Indian sovereignty.

On March 26, 1812, Thomas Meredith, "a respectable old man traveling with his family to Mississippi Territory was murdered on the post road," one of several murders by Creeks of Americans traveling through Indian country that spring.[19] The murder of Thomas Meredith became a high-profile violent symbol of the growing rift between the United States and the Native American nations within its borders. Like other attacks on American citizens in Tennessee and Georgia, the robberies and murders of travelers on the Federal Road were symptomatic of Creek opposition to settlers in their hunting territory and American roads cut through the heart of their country. The attacks on travelers—and resulting punishments of the perpetrators by the Creek leadership—contributed directly to the outbreak of the Creek War of 1813–14.

According to Hawkins, "Thomas Meredith, son of the deceased, who was an eye witness says 'There was murder commited on the body of Thomas Meredith Senior at Kettoma [actually, Pinchona] Creek by Maumouth and others who appeared to be in Liquor, that is Maumouth himself but not the others. The company was all on the other side of the Creek except my father and an other old man. They fell on him without interruption and killed him dead, as he was trying to make his escape in a canoe, and sorely wounded the other with knives & sticks so much that I fear we shall have to bury him on the way.'" Hawkins added that Sam Moniac, "a half breed of large property who keeps entertainment on the road, at whose house Meredith is buried, calls it an 'accident.'"[20]

The Creeks at that time generally considered violent acts carried out under the influence of alcohol to be accidents, not intentional crimes. However, by 1812 the Creek National Council was being pressured by the US government, through its agent Benjamin Hawkins, to accept American legal norms, which held a murderer, whether drunk or sober, responsible for murder. And therefore the National Council had Maumouth and his friends executed for their attack on Meredith and his companion.[21]

Despite the notoriety of the Meredith murder, it had little immediate impact on travel along the Federal Road. Ten days afterward, Hawkins reported, "our road is crowded with travelers, six waggons, 4 carts, 12 chairs and 90 persons passed here today."[22] Over the course of the next year, however, growing Creek discontent with the Americans and with their own leaders coincided with a religious revival among the Creeks known as the Red Stick movement.

The result was civil war in the Creek Nation. By June 1813, Americans living on the borders of the Creek Nation feared the Red Stick uprising would turn into a general war along the entire American frontier. On June 2, General James Wilkinson of the US Army was traveling to Georgia on the Federal Road with his family when he stopped "near Macnac's" to compose a quick note to be conveyed to Hawkins by post rider. Wilkinson had received disturbing news from the Speaker of the Creek National Council, who was besieged by Red Sticks at Tuckabatchee and requested assistance from the Americans. The general and his party made it safely through the nation to Georgia, but they must have been among the last travelers to stop at Moniac's house on the road.[23]

Soon afterward Moniac, as he later recalled, "went up to my house on the road, and found some Indians camped near it whom I tried to avoid, but could not. An Indian came to me, who goes by the name of High Headed Jim. . . . He shook hands with me and immediately began to tremble and jerk in every part of his frame, and the very calves of his legs would be convulsed."[24] High Headed Jim, an adherent of the new religious movement, thought he could discern unbelievers, like Samuel Moniac, by this violent reaction to their touch. Within days of the encounter, Moniac's plantation on the Alabama River and his house on the Federal Road lay in ashes, destroyed by Red Stick Creeks, who included his brother, sister, and brother-in-law.[25]

Historical sources and archaeological investigation of Samuel Moniac's place on the Federal Road provide some clues as to its appearance and the nature of accommodations at that early era.[26] Because he participated actively alongside the American army in the ensuing Red Stick War against many of his relatives and countrymen, Moniac successfully petitioned Congress for compensation for property he lost during that conflict. Moniac was one of the wealthiest Creeks of his era, and his river plantation was among the largest in the Creek Nation. Yet he did not live ostentatiously, and most of his stated wealth consisted of his investments in livestock and enslaved Africans.

Unfortunately, his itemized inventory of property destroyed by the Red Stick Creeks does not distinguish between the two locations, so river plantation

8

[Doc. No. 200.]

I, Gilbert C. Russell, late a Colonel in the Army of the United States, do hereby certify that it was well understood, that the first authentic and accurate information which was received of the hostile intentions of the Creek Indians, was from Mr. Samuel Manac, who, some time in the Summer of 1813, went to the house of the Honorable Henry Toulmin, one of the Judges for the Mississippi Territory, and gave an account, on oath, of the conduct of the unfriendly Creeks, and of what he had learnt relative to their hostile intentions against the citizens of the United States; which was communicated by the Judge to the commanding officer of the Seventh Military District, and I believe, to Governor Holmes. I further certify, that, since that time, I have had the best opportunity of being acquainted with the conduct of Mr. Manac; that I knew it to have been uniformly faithful and loyal; and that the great losses he has sustained, have principally, if not entirely, been in consequence of his attachment to peace, and to the interest of the United States.

GILBERT C. RUSSELL.

The undersigned, Gilbert C. Russell, late a Colonel in the Army of the United States, John T. Wirt, late a Captain and Assistant Deputy Quartermaster General, and John M. Davies, late a Captain and Assistant Inspector General, in the Army aforesaid, do hereby certify, that we are personally acquainted with the foregoing account, that he is famed for integrity and attachment to truth and honesty, and that, in our opinion, his oath is entitled to as much credit as that of any other man.

GILBERT C. RUSSELL,
JNO. T. WIRT,
JNO. M. DAVIES.

(C.)

STATEMENT of property destroyed by the hostile Creek Indians, owned by Captain Samuel Manac, a friendly half breed, during the war between the United States and the Creek tribe of Indians.

Cash taken from dwelling house	$190 00
Flora, negro woman, aged 44 years	300 00
Nancy, child of Flora, do 22 do	400 00
Benjamin, son of Flora, do 28 do	400 00
Punce, negro man, do 50 do	300 00
George, negro boy, do 12 do	250 00
Stephen, negro man, do 28 do	400 00
Louis, negro man, do 45 do	300 00
Cyrus, negro man, do 50 do	300 00
50 head of horses, different kinds and ages	2,050 00
700 head of cattle, customary proportion of ages	4,200 00

[Doc. No. 200.]

48 head of goats and sheep	$240 0
200 head of hogs, common average of ages	860 0
2000 pounds coffee, at 25 cents	500 0
200 pounds sugar, at 25 cents	50 0
32 gallons whiskey, at 150 cents	48 0
30 pounds of lead, at 25 cents	7 5
8 do gunpowder, at 75 cents	6 0
3 bar shear ploughs	18 0
3 shovel ploughs	9 0
15 weeding hoes	15 0
15 axes	45 0
1 wagon	80 0
16 reap hooks, at 125 cents	20 0
1 broad axe	4 0
1 tenon saw	3 0
2 hand saws	8 0
2 foot adzes	4 0
5 augers, assorted	1 7
2 fuzes, at $30	60 0
1 riding saddle	30 0
1 horse mill burnt	75 0
Cotton gin house and machinery burnt	220 0
12 house chairs	9 0
8 spinning wheels	24 0
1 table and bedstead	10 0
2 feather beds	45 0
Weaving looms	45 0
Dwelling house	230 0
500 barrels corn	500 0
50 pounds beeswax	12 5
2000 pounds cotton	40 0
30 pounds wool, at 25 cents	7 5
3 trunks, at $5	15 0
2 large japanned sugar canisters, at $3	6 0
1 grind stone	4 0
2 dozen earthen plates	6 0
10 iron pots	15 7
3 Dutch ovens	10 0
2 dozen cups and saucers	6 0
3 demijohns	9 0
1 barrel salt	6 0
10 mauling wedges	20 0
6 grubbing hoes	18 0
3 large froes	4 5
40 bushels wheat, at $1 50	60 0
House on the Federal Road	30 0
1 boat	25 0
12 pad locks	12 0
3 smoothing planes	4 5

2

Page from Sam Moniac's postwar claim for compensation for losses during the Creek War. H.R. Doc. No. 200, 20th Congress, 1st Sess.

and Federal Road house furnishings and equipment are intermingled in a single list. However, it is logical to surmise some of his large quantities of coffee, sugar, and whiskey were lost at the house on the road. The lists of cooking utensils (ten iron pots, two Dutch ovens, four tin kettles) and food-serving vessels (two dozen earthen plates, two dozen cups and saucers, half a dozen tumblers, half a dozen tin cups) are surprisingly sparse, considering the size of his plantation household, with over thirty slaves, plus relatives, employees, and travelers stopping nightly along the road. The mention of just one bedstead and two feather beds suggests that travelers had to carry their own bedding. The meager collection of artifacts found during archaeological excavations at the Federal Road residence includes small quantities of pottery—some made by Creek Indian women, but most imported from England—a few unclenched nails, and some cast iron kettle parts, all consistent with spartan accommodations for travelers.

Moniac's "Statement of property destroyed" does tell us something more. His "Dwelling House," valued at $230, was evidently his principal residence located at the river plantation, where he had $190 in cash and where his cotton gin house and machinery, worth $220, were burned. Far down the inventory, with a $6 barrel of salt and two corkscrews worth 50 cents, was his "House on the Federal Road" valued at $30.

Judging by its low valuation, this was, almost certainly, a log house, perhaps a dogtrot-style of log house that was becoming popular at that era in the region, among Creeks as well as Americans. The unavailability of sawn planks at the Federal Road house to construct a coffin, noted by Peggy Dow in 1811, and the archaeological find of unclenched nails strengthens the impression of a simple log structure.

One historical reference indicates that Moniac had cow pens in the vicinity of his house on the Federal Road. Creek-owned cattle usually roamed free in the woods, foraging at will for much of the year. Because unfenced cattle would damage crops, most wealthy Creeks kept their cattle at some considerable distance from the major settlements, which probably partially explains the isolated locations of both of Moniac's residences. Cow pens had small fenced enclosures where the normally free-ranging cattle could be rounded up as needed. Thomas Woodward, in a reminiscence written in 1858, recalled Moniac having a cow pen "on the Pinchong creek," referring to Pinchona Creek, where Meredith was murdered, near Moniac's house on the Federal Road. Woodward, Moniac, William Weatherford, and some others went on a cow hunt there in the summer of 1814, as the Red Stick war came to a close, to find food for the destitute and starving Upper Creeks.[27]

THREE

FROM WAR TO STATEHOOD

With the defeat in March 1814 of a large Red Stick force at Tohopeka or Horseshoe Bend by Andrew Jackson's army, the Creek War ended except for continued skirmishing near the coast by a few hundred recalcitrant Red Sticks. During the war, civilian travel on the US mail route and wagon road had essentially come to a halt. Apart from a few intrepid dispatch riders (including Zachariah McGirth, who had briefly considered contracting with Joseph Wheaton to carry the mail back in 1806), few Americans risked their lives to cross the Creek Nation during wartime. The road mainly functioned as a conduit for American armies marching into the nation. Samuel Moniac guided General Ferdinand Claiborne's forces up the road to attack the Red Stick stronghold of Holy Ground in December 1813. General John Floyd's Georgia militia made two forays along the road from the east in November 1813 and January 1814, followed by a Carolina militia army in mid-April. Those invading American forces built forts—Forts Claiborne and Deposit in the south and Mitchell, Hull, Bainbridge, Burrows, and Decatur in the east—that remained important landmarks for years to come. With the formal conclusion of hostilities by the Treaty of Fort Jackson, signed August 9, 1814, the Creek Nation ceded 21,086,793 acres of land to the Americans, retaining only that portion of the Federal Road from the Creek Agency to Fort Mitchell on the Chattahoochee River and westward to Line Creek (the modern boundary between Macon and Montgomery counties in Alabama). About half of the area that would become Alabama suddenly opened for American settlement. With the Federal Road again safe for travel by Americans, immigration soared.[1]

Toward the end of the nineteenth century, Margaret Eades Austill, who had been a young girl during the Creek War, reminisced about those heady days

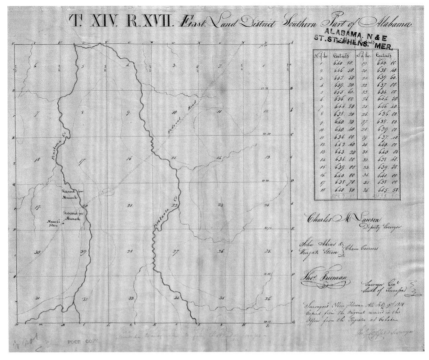

US Surveyor General Thomas Freeman's circa 1816–17 plat for Township 14 N, Range 17 E, show-
ing the location of Samuel Moniac's house on the Federal Road, east of Pinchona Creek, where
Thomas Meredith was murdered in 1812 by Maumouth. Courtesy General Land Office, Bureau of
Land Management, US Department of the Interior, Washington, DC.

of her childhood, the "last of [Eighteen] Fourteen," when "all the people were
gay, money was plenty, and the people were pouring in by the thousands." The
land rush that ensued came to be known as "Alabama Fever," a scramble for
lands newly acquired by the US government that were to be surveyed and sold
to prospective farmers, or in many cases to speculators, as quickly as possible
to pay down the country's debt incurred during the War of 1812. A key figure
of the period was Thomas Freeman, US Surveyor General for this region of
Mississippi Territory and for Alabama Territory from 1817 to 1819. Freeman
directed a team of assistants in laying out the townships, ranges, and mile-
square sections in the initial survey of public lands, which included all of the
lands recently ceded by the Creeks. The township plats from this first official
public land survey—maps generally known as the Freeman plats—provide
an invaluable and accurate description of the landscape, including in many

The home of George Tunstall, built in 1820, near the Federal Road. Tunstall was the brother-in-law of David Tate, Alexander McGillivray's nephew. The Tate and Tunstall families lived in the area, which briefly became the site of Cantonment Montpelier. Only archaeological traces remain of that military installation, built in early 1817 as part of the effort to end Indian disturbances. Tunstall's home is now a private residence. Courtesy of the Historic American Buildings Survey, Library of Congress.

cases the route of the Federal Road, on the eve of American settlement in southwestern Alabama.[2]

Soon after the war, Samuel Moniac rebuilt his house on the Federal Road, although precisely when remains uncertain, as is the duration of his reoccupation. Historian Karl Davis thought Moniac lost his place on the road "in 1816 in part because of anti-Indian attitudes prevailing in the area." The Freeman survey plat showing "Manack's Store" was drawn in 1816 or 1817. Moniac apparently still owned his place there in 1818 when he brought "twenty or more" Creek hunters to the aid of state militia gathering at Burnt Corn Spring to defend American settlements against the depredations of Savannah Jack, a renegade who was committing murders along the Federal Road.[3]

There is also a mention of the "path from Manacs" at that time. However, Maxmillian C. Armstrong's service as postmaster of the local post office at "Manacks" late in 1818 suggests the name by then referred to an American settlement that had formed around the old Federal Road station. The departure of Moniac and his family probably occurred no later than 1819, when death threats against all Creeks still occupying ceded lands prompted the territorial militia to escort frightened Creeks into the Nation.[4]

By the time Adam Hodgson, an English traveler, passed through on his way south to Mobile in 1820, he made no mention of Moniac or his house of entertainment, which had featured so prominently in the Federal Road's early years. Hodgson's account does provide a good description of the original prairie environment and sticky chalk soils of the Pintlala area:

> We soon opened on some of the beautiful prairies which you have frequently seen described, and which, as they were not large, reminded me of our meadows in the well wooded parts of England. As travellers, however, we paid dearly for the advantages offered to the landholders by the rich soil over which we were passing. Our road, which had hitherto been generally excellent for travelling on horseback, became as wretchedly bad; and we passed through three swamps, which I feared would ruin our horses. . . . These swamps are ten times more formidable than even the flooded creeks, over two of which, in less than three miles, we had this day to have our horses swum by Indians, whose agility in the water is beautiful. The traveller himself is either conveyed over in a boat, or, if the creek is very narrow, crosses it on a large tree, which has been so dexterously felled as to fall across and form a tolerable bridge. We slept that night at a poor cabin just erected.[5]

Immense changes to the cultural landscape occurred along the Federal Road during the period from 1814 to 1820. One direct consequence of the Creek War and the War of 1812 was a militarization of the Gulf Coast region. The Treaty of Ghent ending the War of 1812 failed to resolve many of the war's causes. Tensions ran high along the Canadian border as well as in the south, where Florida remained in Spanish hands. Numerous Red Stick Creeks and Seminoles found refuge there and remained actively opposed to the United States. Continued British efforts to support their former Indian allies in Florida raised concerns in the United States that the invasion repelled at New Orleans in 1815 had not extinguished British aspirations for the Gulf Coast. In response, the Americans concentrated one-quarter of their postwar army in just two locations, on the New York–Ontario border and immediately adjacent to the border of Spanish Florida, north and west of Pensacola.

In 1814, as General Jackson prepared for an invasion of Spanish Florida, the US military abandoned Fort Stoddert and established Fort Montgomery east of the Mobile-Tensaw delta, about two miles from the site of ill-fated Fort Mims. According to Jackson's topographical engineer, Major Howell Tatum, the Thirty-Ninth US Infantry Regiment, commanded by Lieutenant

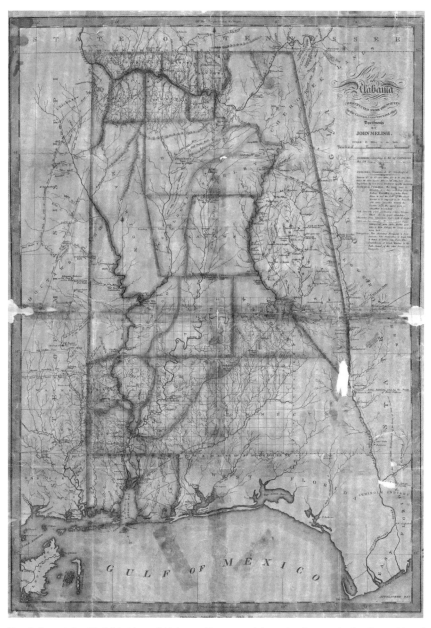

Detail from John Melish's *Map of Alabama Constructed from the Surveys in the General Land Office and Other Documents* (Philadelphia, 1818), showing Forts Stoddert, Mims, Montgomery, and Claiborne in relation to the "Federal Road to Georgia." Courtesy Alabama Department of Archives and History.

Colonel Thomas Hart Benton, began construction in August of a stockade fort on Holmes's Hill "as a means of giving greater security to the settlers on the East side of the Mobile & alabama rivers." By the end of October, Jackson there assembled his army of 4,400 men for the march on Spanish Pensacola, which he besieged and captured. Although diplomatic exigencies forced his withdrawal from Florida, the US Army retained a significant presence at Fort Montgomery until 1818, and from 1817 until 1820 at Cantonment Montpelier, a few miles up the Federal Road.[6]

Besides the perceived geopolitical threat posed by a foreign-held colony on the southern US border, sporadic hostilities continued for some years along the southern reaches of the Federal Road, which justified a continued strong military presence. These sporadic attacks on settlers, some of them fatal, were generally the work of small, roving, isolated bands of Red Stick Creeks displaced by the Treaty of Fort Jackson. In February 1816 two settlers named Johnson and Magasky were killed near Fort Claiborne; in July 1817 a Mr. Glass was murdered at Burnt Corn Spring; and, most famously, many members of the Ogle and Stroud families were murdered farther up the road in 1818.

All were attributed to renegade Creeks. After each event, territorial militia were called on to capture or kill the perpetrators, who kept the frontier in turmoil. Indeed, these hostile Creek actions were part of the larger unrest in Florida among refugee Creeks and Seminoles. After the last of these outrages, Colonel Sam Dale constructed a small stockade with two blockhouses around a settler's cabin at a place thereafter called Fort Dale, just northwest of modern-day Greenville. In July 1818, citizens of Alabama Territory seized and hanged five captive Red Stick Creeks (including the famous Paddy Welch) being transferred by the US military from Fort Claiborne to Fort Montgomery via the Federal Road. That failure of American justice caused most Creeks remaining in the ceded lands to flee to the Creek Nation.[7]

By the time of statehood, Indian troubles on the ceded land had largely ended. As settlers poured into the region—across the remnants of the Creek Nation—small settlements, farms, sizeable plantations devoted to cotton production, and churches proliferated. Even though delivery of US mail had been the original motivation for creation of the Federal Road, creating a dependable and rapid mail system remained an elusive goal in the early years. After the Creek War, however, mail service quickly became routine. A "Postal-Route Advertisement" dated June 20, 1818, lists two routes (designated 229 and 231) on the original Federal Road, as well as several others on popular branches of the road to Fort Claiborne, St. Stephens, and Blakeley. Route 229 ran "from Coweta, by Fort Bainbridge, Fort Hull, Tuckabatchy, Line Creek, Pleasant

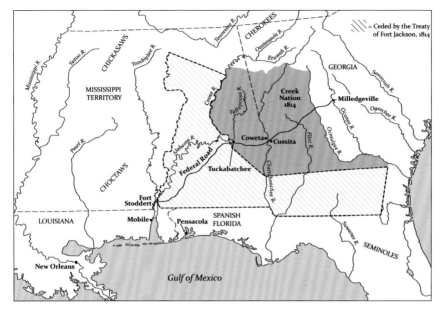

The Federal Road and Treaty of Fort Jackson cession.

Level, Philadelphia and Manacs, Whetstone Hill, 141 miles, twice a week," leaving Coweta on the Chattahoochee at 2:00 P.M. every Tuesday and Friday and arriving at Whetstone Hill by 6:00 P.M. on Friday and Monday. Compared to the timetable envisioned in 1805 by Postmaster General Granger, this relaxed schedule better suited real-life conditions on the post road. Normalization of mail service in postwar Alabama led to establishment of eight post offices along the Federal Road and its major branches by 1819; in 1805 there had been just two, at St. Stephens and Fort Stoddert.[8] By 1828 additional post offices operated at Bainbridge, Creek Path, Greenville, Longmire's Store, Suggsville, and Tensaw, while Manack's had moved to Pintlala.[9]

POST OFFICE	POSTMASTER	FIRST RETURN
Line Creek	James Abercrombie	July 17, 1819
Manack's	Maxmillian C. Armstrong	August 21, 1818
Fort Dale	John Herbert	October 12, 1818
Burnt Corn Spring	William James	October 26, 1817
Fort Claiborne	John Watkins	July 2, 1818
St. Stephens	John G. Lyon	November 1, 1816
Fort Stoddert	Harry Toulmin	February 1, 1819
Blakeley	Samuel Haines	April 21, 1818

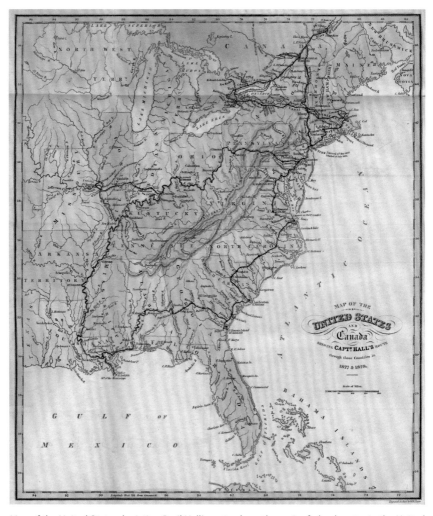

Map of the United States depicting Basil Hall's route along the major federal routes in the United States. Courtesy of the Alabama Department of Archives and History.

Despite the name "Federal Road," maintenance expenses for the road remained the responsibility of the federal government only through the territorial period. Between 1806 and 1809, creation of a horse path had cost the United States $5,500 of the $13,800 appropriated by Congress, although of course that initial effort was a failure.[10] The task of road building fell to US Army troops when other means proved ineffective, but figures for the US Army's costs to convert the horse path to a wagon road in 1810 and 1811 have not been found. In 1817, the secretary of war directed $5,000 to David Mitchell, Benjamin Hawkins's replacement at the Creek Agency, for building and keeping in repair the road and bridges between Fort Hawkins in Georgia and old Fort Stoddert, with an equal amount allocated to private contractors. State and federal officials also considered plans to improve the route by shortening the distance or shifting the road to avoid swamps and major river crossings.

None of this happened, and even simple bridge building proved nearly impossible to accomplish, because, according to Mitchell, "the people in that quarter are so much engaged in clearing land and making Plantations that they will not for any reasonable compensation detach their hands from that object." No wonder Israel Pickens wrote home from St. Stephens in 1818 that he had just endured "a tedious and unpleasant journey with my family over the almost impassable road which leads from Georgia here."[11]

Once Alabama achieved statehood late in 1819, most expenditures for maintenance of the Federal Road fell to state and county officials. An early act of the Alabama legislature specified how public roads were to be maintained.

> Chapter 5: An Act to reduce into one the several Acts concerning Roads, Bridges, Ferries, and Highways.—Passed December 21, 1820.
>
> Sec. 1. *Be it enacted* . . . That all public roads and highways in the several counties of this state, that have been laid out or appointed by virtue of any act of the general assembly heretofore made, or by virtue of any act of court, are hereby declared to be public roads; . . .
>
> Sec. 3. *Be it further enacted*, That all free white male persons, between eighteen and forty-five years of age, and all male slaves, and other persons of colour over eighteen and under fifty years of age, shall be liable, and it is hereby made their duty to work on, clear out, and repair the public roads of this state, under such provisions and regulations as are herein after made: *Provided nevertheless*, That no licensed ministers of the gospel, or instructors of public and private schools, shall be liable to work on public roads.[12]

Enforcement of these and later provisions became the purview of county road commissions by the 1830s.

Harriet Martineau painted by Richard Evans, ca. 1834. Courtesy of the
National Portrait Gallery, London.

FOUR

TRAVELING THE
FEDERAL ROAD

Although poorly maintained, the Federal Road saw heavy traffic by government officials, businessmen, tourists, and especially emigrants intent on building new homes in Alabama or points beyond. Fortunately for us, many well-educated travelers published accounts of their adventures on the Federal Road. They universally cursed the road, particularly the segment through the Creek Nation, and decried its dangers and discomforts. It was, Harriet Martineau concluded, "as bad as roads could be."[1] Martineau, an Englishwoman who toured the United States in the 1830s, was one of many (mostly European) travelers whose published travel writings critiqued American society and culture. A Unitarian social theorist who abhorred slavery, she was particularly attuned to the conditions of women and children. Thomas Hamilton, a retired British officer whose military exploits informed his popular novel *The Youth and Manhood of Cyril Thornton*, provided an acerbic account of 1820s America and delighted in reciting the difficulties he encountered while traveling. With *Letters from Alabama*, American Anne Royall turned to travel journalism as a means of financial support when her late husband's annulled will left her a penniless widow. Tried and convicted in Washington, DC, as a "public nuisance, a common brawler and a common scold," she paid her $10 fine and continued traveling and writing, pumping out ten accounts in her lifetime.[2]

Many who embraced the travel genre were not simply professional writers, but writers whose careers required travel. The Englishman George Featherstonhaugh (pronounced "Fanshaw"), whose fame rested largely on his expertise as a geologist, resided in America, where he founded and edited the *Monthly American Journal of Geology and Natural Science* beginning in 1831.

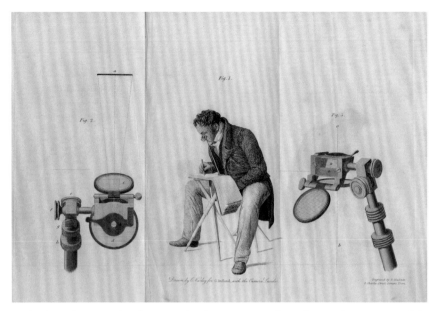

Basil Hall used a camera lucida as an aid in drawing scenes during his travels. *Description of the Camera Lucida: An Instrument for Drawing in True Perspective . . . to which is added . . . A letter on the use of the Camera by Capt. Basil Hall.* London, 1830. Courtesy of the Beinecke Rare Book and Manuscript Library, Yale University.

His travels along the Federal Road in 1835 were part of his geologic survey of America. Featherstonhaugh later served as British consul at Le Havre and helped King Louis Philippe escape the 1848 French Revolution.[3] Basil Hall, a Scottish naval officer, author, and scientist, published numerous works on his travels to Latin America and China as well as in North America along the Federal Road. His wife Margaret's own impressions, in letters to her sister, found their way into print in 1931.[4] *Lafayette en Amérique en 1824 et 1825* documented the progress of no doubt the most famous traveler of all those who endured the Federal Road, as memorialized by General Lafayette's personal secretary, Auguste Levasseur.[5]

Tyrone Power, an Irish actor and playwright, based *Impressions of America* on his tour from 1833 to 1835.[6] "Old Sol"—as the humorist and actor Solomon Franklin Smith was known due to his penchant for playing old patriarchs in various performances—managed a theatrical company that toured the South for many years.[7] Phineas Taylor Barnum was relatively new to "show business" when he crossed the Creek Country via the Federal Road in 1837. Like the artist John James Audubon, who covered the same ground that year, P. T.

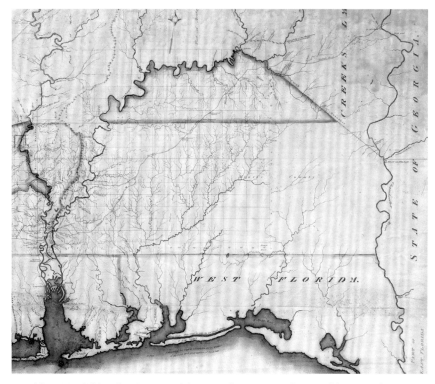

Detail from Maxfield Ludlow's *A Map of the State of Louisiana, with parts of the State of Mississippi and Alabama Territory*, ca. 1816. Courtesy of the Historic New Orleans Collection, accession number 1939.2.

Barnum left us his impressions of Indian Removal. Audubon recorded his thoughts in private letters, as did the southern literary giant William Gilmore Simms, whose works include romanticized fiction inspired by the fate of the southeastern Indians.[8]

The travelogues and epistles of these and other nineteenth-century writers are invaluable today for their honest, often critical, assessments of life in early Alabama. One reviewer thought Adam Hodgson's 1824 book "desultory," but even the least accomplished writers documented the names of people and places they encountered along the Federal Road.[9] The best of these accounts, by educated and frequently well-connected people, contain revealing observations of the cultural differences of those they encountered on their journeys. Their wide travels, education, and perceptive eyes enabled them to write richly descriptive and sometimes witty narratives. Together their works comprise

an entertaining evaluation of life and times along the Federal Road, including eyewitness accounts of the changing nature of Creek society, particularly
the rise of slave-holding among the Indians, as well as the new slave society
devoted to cotton agriculture that rapidly developed in the state of Alabama.

By the 1820s, the nature of the Federal Road was changing rapidly under
the wheels of thousands of travelers' vehicles, which wore away at the simple
earthen roadbed. The original horse path was intentionally narrow, no more
than a few feet wide. In some habitats a broader gash in the tree canopy would
let sunlight penetrate the forest floor, causing a proliferation of entangling
vines and other undergrowth that would quickly make the path impassable.
While the heavier traffic that traversed the wider wagon road effectively beat
back encroaching vegetation, the influx of wheeled vehicles also created ruts
that soon led to severe erosion on slopes. Even on relatively level terrain the
road eventually became entrenched in many places, replicating the "sunken"
lanes or "holloways" that famously characterize the Natchez Trace and other
ancient roadways around the world.[10]

In Alabama, travelers observed changes in the landscape in the upper
section of the Federal Road that corresponded to differences in the underly-
ing geology. Leaving the Chattahoochee valley, the soil was "sandy and poor,
it bore nothing but pine trees." Many noted the open forest along the high
pine ridges as they left Fort Mitchell. One traveler was particularly struck by
longleaf pine "trees of the noblest height, and just so far apart that horsemen
might gallop in any direction without difficulty."[11] Proceeding westward the
subsoil turned to "reddish-yellow" clay and pine forests gave way to hardwood
stands of oak and hickory. Retired Member of Parliament James Buckingham
observed, in 1839, as the sandy high ridge road descended into clay soils of the
bottomlands, so too did the quality of the road. A "mere pathway through and
around standing trees" in wet weather became a "waxy" quagmire.[12]

In such situations, travelers—if they were lucky—became acquainted with
a "a sort of pavement formed of logs of trees, or what is called in America, a
'corduroy road.'"[13] Even on relatively high and dry level ground, the effects of
traffic and lack of maintenance turned the road rough and bumpy, making a
carriage ride, as graphically described by Adam Hodgson in 1820, "a perpet-
ual undulation."[14] On his journey from Columbus to Montgomery, Thomas
Hamilton learned how trees felled by the wind and stumps of trees left in the
roadbed presented serious and frequent obstacles. In the case of the former,
"the united exertions of the passengers" were called on time and again to hoist
fallen trees from the road before proceeding.[15] Between the hills, the slippery

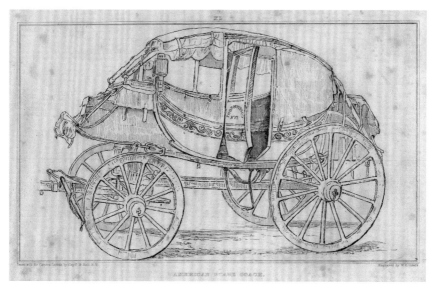

American Stage Coach, drawn by Basil Hall using the camera lucida. Courtesy of the Alabama Department of Archives and History.

roads, and the many impediments they faced, even by the late 1820s travelers "could only creep along in the most tedious manner" and often "on foot" when conditions became so rough that riding was impossible, or the condition of a broken carriage mandated such an outcome.[16]

Thomas Hamilton summed up the feelings of most of those who traversed the Federal Road when he wrote, in 1831, the section of road from Columbus to Montgomery was "positively, comparatively, and superlatively, the *very worst* I have ever travelled in the whole course of my peregrinations. The ruts were axle-deep, and huge crevices occasionally occurred, in which, but for great strategy on the part of the coachman, the vehicle must have been engulfed."[17]

In a new country, where highway maintenance ranged from slim to none, travelers found the road very primitive indeed. With the passage of time, "improvements" such as bridges, ferries, and causeways across swamps ostensibly made travel somewhat easier. With a sparse population, maintenance of the road was difficult, and this was particularly true within the bounds of the Creek Nation. In the late 1820s, government mail contractors reportedly hired the Creek Chief Tuskina to clear the road of obstructions. When he was then refused payment and treated with "derision," Tuskina stopped a stage, which was transporting "famous German rope-dancers," and threatened the driver with "a common jack-knife."[18]

Even after transfer of the Creek domain to Alabama in the late 1830s and early 1840s, as population swelled, road maintenance remained minimal. Traveling from Columbus to Montgomery in 1839, James Buckingham's stage broke down twice in the thirty miles east of Montgomery. The coach was literally shaken to pieces. As he explained, "the corduroy ridges of round logs extending sometimes for upward of a mile in continuity, and so violently shaking the coach, that though it was nearly new, and built with great strength, it broke down with us in the middle of the road." Passengers had to get out and walk in the rain. His coach was repaired "by the assistance of [enslaved] negroes sent from the farm, with poles of wood, and such rude tools as they could obtain for the purpose."[19] He knew there was little incentive for the locals to maintain or improve the road. For, as he observed, "a very little labour from each adjoining plantation would put these roads in excellent condition; but the reason assigned for this not being applied is, that every planter considers himself only a temporary occupant of the plantation on which he is settled." Each one was eager to sell and move west at the first opportunity and thus unwilling to expend personal resources to improve public roads.[20]

Stream and river crossings were particularly dreaded and potentially hazardous, especially at night. Narrow and sluggish flows could be forded easily enough, but bridges, boats, or ferries were required in periods of high water or in the case of larger streams and rivers. Until their forced removal from Alabama, Indians assisted at crossings for a fee, as was their right by treaty. Indians operated ferries, assisted in swimming horses across rivers, maintained the bridges, and served as guides through swamps during the night.[21] Some of the Federal Road's other economic opportunities attracted Indians, called "Ninny-pask-ulgees," to the roadside. *Nene* is the Muskogee word for road, and the modern Muskogee term for street sweeper is *nene-espaskv*, probably derived from the days when Indians were hired by federal authorities to keep the road clear. In addition, nearby Indian camps were frequently visited by travelers in search of supplies and assistance.[22]

The raccoon bridges of William Bartram's era still came in handy in emergencies, and travelers admired how Indians "dexterously felled" trees across a stream to "form a tolerable bridge."[23] But by the 1820s, log or plank bridges were the norm. In some cases, these crude bridges spanned swampy locations. Tyrone Power encountered a bridge of "loose" planks "a quarter of a mile in length, unguarded by a rail or bulwark of the slightest kind" and "overhung

Basil Hall's sketch of a *Bridge of Split Logs across the Pachelagee Creek in Georgia on the Federal Road 29th March 1828*. Courtesy of the Lilly Library, Indiana University, Bloomington, Indiana.

Marlow Ferry Crossing, Baldwin County, operating on the Fish River around 1920, displays many of the characteristics of early ferries. Courtesy of the Doris Rich Collection, Negative Number Rich-4. The Doy Leale McCall Rare Book and Manuscript Library, University of South Alabama.

by the rank growth of the jungle through which it was laid."[24] In some cases, Indians might be paid "liberally" to help travelers traverse a "broken-down log-bridge that was dangerous in some places."[25] Since the Creeks were responsible for bridge upkeep, travelers had little choice but to grudgingly pay the requested fees or search for alternative routes.

At major river crossings, ferries tethered by stout tow ropes to either shore were pulled across by horse or human.[26] Generally, these crude ferries were no more than rafts, referred to as "flats" or "floats."[27] Generally, carriages floated across on the ferry, while horses swam the river, as sometimes did the passengers, although more commonly they took to small boats. Still, a river crossing could take hours.[28] Convincing horses to take the plunge was no trivial matter, and ferrymen employed a variety of persuasions, including "singing" or whooping to frighten horse teams into deep and sometimes raging rivers.[29]

Swamps, especially the largest ones, could be treacherous. Adam Hodgson's 1820 account of his travels southwest of Line Creek, in Alabama Territory, well describes the nature of the Federal Road through the chalky soils of the Black Belt. As pine forest gave way to oaks and prairies, he encountered three swamps,

> about a mile long each; but we estimated the fatigue of crossing any of them as equivalent to at least 15 or 20 miles of common travelling. They were overshadowed with beautiful but entangling trees, without any regular track through the verdure which covered the thick clay in which our horses frequently stuck, as much at a loss where to take the next step, as how to extricate themselves from the last.
>
> Sometimes they had to scramble out of the deep mire upon the trunk of a fallen tree, from which they could not descend without again sinking on the other side.
>
> Sometimes we were so completely entangled in the vines, that we were compelled to dismount to cut our way out of the vegetable meshes in which we seemed to be entrapped. These swamps are ten times more formidable than even the flooded creeks.[30]

No doubt the most memorable river crossing in the history of the Federal Road occurred in 1825. During his tour of the southern states, the Marquis de Lafayette's party arrived at the Chattahoochee River escorted by dignitaries from Georgia. On the western riverbank, on entering the remaining portion of the Creek Nation in the state of Alabama, awaited a delegation of Alabama and Creek dignitaries to welcome the last surviving general of the American

The Marquis de Lafayette. Courtesy of Library of Congress.

Revolution. A crowd of all ages had turned out to witness the famous visitor's arrival, and, as the ferry landed, Creek men ran forward to greet him. According to Auguste Levasseur, the general's secretary, the Indians "became excited, jumped and danced around him, touched his hands and his clothes with an air of surprise and rapture." Their leader gave "a piercing and long-prolonged cry that was repeated by the entire throng." As General Lafayette began to disembark, "some of the strongest of them took hold of a little cabriolet that we had with us and had the General climb into it, not wanting, they said, their father to set foot on wet soil. The General was carried in this manner in a palanquin up to a certain distance from the riverbank."[31]

Farther down the road Sam Dale, one of the Alabama delegation, reported (via his biographer) that "when we reached the Callabee swamp, usually very

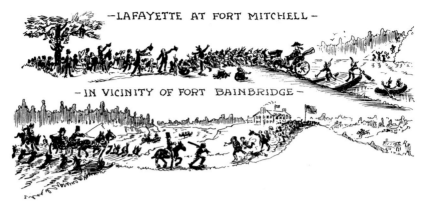

Lafayette crossing the Chattahoochee at Fort Mitchell and on to Fort Bainbridge. Cartoon from the *Montgomery Advertiser*, April 2, 1925, reprinted in *Arrow Points* 10 (May 5, 1925): 61.

bad, the Indians had preceded us, and had laid down poles, and across them heavy transverse logs to prevent them from floating, themselves in the water, and holding down the logs until the procession passed over. They escorted the general to the confines of their territory, evidently regarding him as a great warrior, deserving this spontaneous homage to his fame."[32]

Until the end of the Creek War, horseback remained the primary mode of travel on the Federal Road, but increasingly travelers came on wheels. By this time most were emigrants who planned to resettle on newly acquired Indian lands, and they traveled in an amazing variety of conveyances, "the whole family of wheeled vehicles, innumerable," according to Basil Hall.[33] Adam Hodgson observed in 1820 "a curious collection of sans soucis, sulkies, carts, Jersey waggons, [and] heavy waggons" as well as the more comfortable "light carriage" favored by those of means (which included most of our travel writers).[34]

As demand for transport rose, regular stagecoach services vied for customers. In some cases, the "stage coach" was no more than the wagon contracted for carrying mail.[35] The light carriage mentioned by Hodgson was no doubt the barouche, a carriage on four wheels, with a driver's seat high up front and double facing seats for passengers, usually sporting a folding top for inclement weather. A Jersey wagon was a "humble" four-wheeled conveyance, essentially a box on two axles, without springs, also known as a "dearborn, or carry-all," typically with two seats, a wagon cover, and side curtains.[36] Whatever the vehicle, all were uncomfortable and some nearly defied description. John James Audubon, whose artist's eyes captured the exquisite detail of his avian subjects, could only

Basil Hall's sketch of *Carriage in which we travelled from Darien to Montgomery. With Middleton on the Box. 4th April 1828.* Courtesy of the Lilly Library, Indiana University, Bloomington, Indiana.

classify the vehicle in which he traveled as "a large Barn like Coach."[37] Sometimes, baggage was transported separately, especially during the late 1820s and 1830s, in a large canvas-covered "Pennsylvania road wagon."[38]

Charles Lyell, in 1846, managed to snag a ride on the "better" class of carriage, one "built on a plan almost universal in America, and like those used in some parts of France, with three seats, the middle one provided with a broad leather strap, to lean back upon." Female passengers were given the "best places," while their husbands and other male passengers gallantly filled the remaining seats. Occasionally, one of the men might choose to sit with the driver, but otherwise all remained in the carriage, unless, due to a broken wheel or other misfortune, they were forced to walk. Even while sitting, passengers were active participants in their transportation. Lyell and his fellow passengers "were often called upon, on a sudden, to throw our weight first on the right, and then on the left side, to balance the vehicle and prevent an upset, when one wheel was sinking into a deep rut."[39] Passengers in vehicles without adequate suspension might find themselves "tossed and tumbled" the entire stretch of the Federal Road.[40]

Basil Hall described the coach that carried his wife and him:

> An American stage is more like a French diligence than any thing else. Like that vehicle it carries no outside passengers, except one or two on the box. It has three seats inside, two of which are similar to the front and back seats of an English coach, while the third is placed across the middle from the window to window, or I might say, from door to door, only these stages very seldom have more than one door. Instead of panels, there hang from the roof leather curtains, which, when buttoned down, render it a close carriage; or when rolled up and fastened by straps and buttons to the roof, leave it open all round. This for summer traveling is agreeable enough; but how passengers manage in the severe winters of the north, I do not know; for certainly we found it on many occasions, even in the south, uncomfortably cold. The middle seat is movable on a sort of hinge, that it may be turned, horizontally, out of the way when the door is opened. The three passengers who sit upon it, rest their backs against a stuffed leather strap, permanently buckled to one side of the carriage, and attached to the other side by means of a stout iron hook. These ponderous stages are supported on strong hide straps, in place of steel springs, and all parts are made of great strength, which is absolutely necessary to enable them to bear the dreadful jostling on the miserable roads they have but too frequently the fate to travel over.[41]

For her part, Margaret Hall found travel a test of endurance. Traveling, on average, thirty miles a day in their carriage, she reported that "every bone aches from ill usage." The ceaseless jostling of the carriage was as intolerable as the bad lodgings where they attempted to rest each night. But, she intoned, "what I have felt the great suffering is the dirt that we have to put up with in everything, even in our food."[42]

As traffic increased on the Federal Road, travelers vied for available space on the better carriage lines. The alternative, as Tyrone Power and his equally unfortunate traveling companions found, was to travel on the "*Box*," the rude wagon that carried the mail. And a box it truly was. Power described it as

Lafayette souvenir clothes brush. Travelers found themselves covered with mud and dust. Hence, a clothes brush seemed an appropriate object to commemorate the general's journey through the states. Courtesy Lafayette College.

Hide-covered trunks, often with decorative finishes, were the primary means of transporting personal goods on journeys. A leather covering providing a degree of protection from the elements. Courtesy of the Alabama Department of Archives and History.

"made of rough fir plank, eight feet long by three feet wide, with sides two feet deep: it was fixed firmly on an ordinary coach-axle, with pole &c. The mails and luggage filled the box to overflowing, and on the top of all we were left to, as the driver said, 'fix our four quarters in as leetle [*sic*] time as possible.'" Power, who characterized his fellow travelers as "victims," was mortified that "not the least care having been taken in the disposition of the luggage, our sole care, in fact, was to guard against being jolted off by the movement of the machine; any disposition in favour of ease or comfort was quite out of the question." It was, as Power wrote, a choice "between the Box and the forest," the only recourse being "the travelers' privilege" of grumbling.[43]

Settlers on the way to Alabama commonly traveled in small groups of family members or neighbors, in caravans of two to four wagons. Power described the large, heavy wagons favored by emigrants moving their households as "tilt wagons, long and low-roofed; each laden, first with needful provisions and such household gear as may be considered indispensable; next, over this portion of the freight is stowed the family of the emigrant planter, his wife, and commonly a round squad of white-haired children." Power noted the wagons were "preceded and surrounded by the field slaves, varying in numbers from half a dozen to fifty or sixty, according to the wealth of the proprietor."[44] Such caravans usually made from twelve to fifteen miles per day.[45]

Poor road conditions and rough travel meant frequent breakdowns and the need for repair and replacement of damaged wagon parts. Basil Hall's party was lucky enough to find an English coach maker in Macon, Georgia, when the perch of their carriage broke and needed replacement. Along the Alabama portion of the road, drivers and travelers had to repair their own vehicles or depend on the services and help of innkeepers or residents along the road.

FIVE

TAVERNS AND STAGE STOPS

The earliest way stations operated by James Cornells and Sam Moniac, which played a large role in instigating the Creek War, were soon bypassed in the hustle and bustle of development that followed in the wake of peace. At Burnt Corn Spring, where an American settlement quickly appeared and long remained an important stop on the mail routes to Pensacola and Mobile, Garrett and Susannah Longmire settled in 1816 and operated one of the first hotels on the road.

However, even after the war, American travel and settlement along the Federal Road continued as an irritant to the Creeks. A series of Indian attacks on settlers along the lower stretches of the road between 1816 and 1818 resulted in counterattacks by American militias. With the establishment of the state of Alabama in 1819, and anti-Indian sentiments still running high, Sam Moniac and many other Indians living within the new state boundaries found it prudent to relocate to Creek territory.

Thus, as "Alabama Fever" for the rich newly opened lands drove immigration to new heights and tourism increased, inns and stage stops along the Federal Road were increasingly owned and operated by white proprietors. Most Creeks were reduced to menial jobs and increasing poverty as the new economic and political reality confined them to marginal roles in a rapidly changing world.[1]

Stage stops, inns, taverns, and "stands" offered travelers provisions and lodging all along the Federal Road. Prior to 1820, however, the number of travelers far exceeded available lodging. On the road in 1819, James Campbell's party of sixteen found accommodations for the night of April 27 at "Manacks," near Pintlala Creek, but spent the five nights before and five nights after "camped in the woods." During the 1820s–1840s, the heyday of travel on the road, hotels and taverns changed with the times to meet travelers' needs. Many became famous (or infamous) for their accommodations. Travelers occasionally praised their hosts, but exorbitant charges and primitive conditions elicited many more complaints. Although some hoteliers were accommodating or at least entertaining due to their eccentricities, many more proved cantankerous and stingy. If we believe James Stuart, the latter included "the worst tempered American female" he encountered in three years of extensive travel across North America.[2]

The earliest structures along the road followed traditional native construction styles, but this quickly gave way to rude log and clapboard "huts." "Dog trot" log houses, with central roofed passageways, proved especially popular, even after sawn boards became available for frame construction. Still, skilled carpenters were rare and shoddy construction the norm in the early years. Mud mixed with Spanish moss filled the chinks in log buildings, if the owner bothered to fill them at all. Basil Hall, recalling one of his log accommodations on the road, marveled at "being able, while lying in bed, to thrust my arm between two of the logs into the open air!"[3] With the passage of time, large clapboard inns and taverns replaced small cabins and huts, and a degree of rustic comfort ensued.

Glass windows were virtually unknown, while poorly maintained walls and roofs kept out neither rain nor cold wind. Lack of amenities such as candles, linens, and comfortable bedding was a frequent traveler lament.[4] Guests often shared rooms, sometimes beds, and the close quarters practically guaranteed sleepless nights filled with all manner of unpleasantness. Thin walls meant "the slightest noise or sound made in one room could be distinctly heard in the next . . . cries of some young children, the snoring of the negroes scattered about lying on the floor, the constant barking of several large dogs . . . and the incessant croakings of the frogs, with which every part of these woods abound, made it impossible to sleep."[5] On occasion, the torment was more personal. For in addition to bedbugs endured in an unnamed Indian tavern between Montgomery and Fort Mitchell, Thomas Hamilton discovered that "sleep . . . was impossible, under the incessant attacks of a multitude of blood-suckers, which, flea for man, would have outnumbered the army of Xerxes."[6]

In the post–Creek War era, the raw new town of Columbus, Georgia, was the last major white settlement for travelers heading west through the Creek Nation until they reached Montgomery. Founded in 1828 on the Chattahoochee River, at the fall line near the Creek town of Cussita, Columbus grew

Embryo Town of Columbus on the Chatahoochie, by Basil Hall. Hall wrote that "this Sketch represents the most populous and best cleared part of the city. The other streets were only just marked out by narrow lanes, a yard wide, cut through the brushwood by the surveyors." From *Forty Etchings: From Sketches made with the Camera Lucida in 1827 and 1828 by Captain Basil Hall* (Edinburgh: Cadell, 1829). Courtesy of the Beinecke Rare Book and Manuscript Library, Yale University.

rapidly after the 1826 Treaty of Washington transferred all Creek land claimed by Georgia to that state.

When Basil Hall passed through Columbus in 1828, he counted three hotels, one advertised by a sign nailed to a tree that still stood in the middle of the newly laid-out street. Since no lots had been sold at the time, the recently arrived inhabitants of the town were building their houses "on trucks—a sort of low, strong wheels, such as cannon are supported by—for the avowed purpose of being hurled [hauled] away when the land should be sold."[7] But a sense of permanency soon took hold, and by 1833 there were churches, a post office, and more than 130 wood-frame buildings as well as a few more substantial brick establishments.[8] Harriet Martineau, who visited in 1845, counted five hotels, noted a population of two thousand, and thought the "stores looked creditably stocked." She considered the "thriving, spacious, handsome village, well worth stopping to see."[9]

Martineau did not mention what lay across the Chattahoochee, but Tyrone Power made particular note in 1834 of "Sodom," the "wild-looking village, scattered through the edge of the forest" that sprang up near the Indian town of Coweta.

Sketch of Tustanagee Hopoy or Little Prince by Lukas Vischer, a Swiss traveler. Vischer visited this man, the leading chief of the Lower Creeks, at his home not far from Fort Mitchell. Courtesy Vischer family.

Power declared the inhabitants to be "'minions o' the moon,' outlaws from the neighbouring States," whose illicit business kept them out late. Lawless and bold, they found refuge from the US Marshal in Creek territory and terrorized the local Indians, who were powerless to expel them.[10] In 1821, newly appointed federal agent John Crowell had relocated the Creek Agency to just north of the Federal Road, near the original site of Fort Mitchell. That fort had been built during the Creek War along an old trading path at one of the best Chattahoochee River crossings. A subsequent, smaller Fort Mitchell, built in 1825 during the First Seminole War, would become base of operations in the 1830s for removal of the Creek Indians from Alabama.

Nearby Crowell's Tavern, which went through several hands, mainly served soldiers and had a reputation for noise, poor service, and poorer

Medetuchkt, an Upper Creek Indian student at the Baptist Mission school at Tuckabatchee, 1824. Sketch by Lukas Vischer. Courtesy Vischer family.

accommodations. Thomas Crowell, the Indian agent's brother, operated the tavern from roughly 1825 to 1830, when it became Johnson's Hotel, run by Major James Johnson, who had been the mail carrier between Milledgeville and Montgomery and part owner of a stagecoach line.[11] Dr. Jacob Motte, an army surgeon during the Second Creek War, described Johnson's as nothing more than a "log-house."[12]

Shortly after Crowell's arrival, the Methodist Church built Asbury Mission near the fort, and in 1822 their school opened to Indian children. By 1825, a model farm was likewise in operation. The Reverend Whitman C. Hill, who ran the mission from 1825 to 1828, presided over a cluster of log buildings that housed the pupils. There they learned to read and write, as Hill sought with limited success to convert them to Christianity.[13]

Carl Bernhard, Duke of Saxe-Weimar-Eisenach, stopped at Crowell's Tavern in January 1826 and found himself "lodged in an airy out-house of clapboards, without a ceiling, and windows without glass." Opined the acerbic duke, "we were accommodated with freer circulation than would have fallen to our lot in a German barn." By this time the army post, a square enclosure of pickets, with blockhouses at the corners, had been regarrisoned, due to trouble over the infamous and illegal Treaty of Indian Springs (1825), whereby William McIntosh signed away all Creek Nation lands east of the Chattahoochee River. Bernhard and his traveling companions, Colonel John E. Wool (inspector general of the US Army) and Temple Bowdoin (a former British army officer), shared drinks with American officers at the tavern and were "much pleased with their society."[14]

Anne Royall, who arrived at Fort Mitchell in 1830, had the opposite reaction to the seasoned and urbane military men. Insulted by the soldiers, whom she dubbed "a parcel of poltroons," and annoyed by the raucous tavern, she found comfort in her lodging, tended by two Indian women: a cook and chambermaid. This retreat to female company "fairly restored me to youth . . . a real paradise." Royall stayed in one of the "little huts, adjoining the tavern," which had "two good beds in it, a table and a few chairs." Her Creek landlady, Mrs. Johnson, provided her with tea, pen and ink, and a candle so the writer could work in the evening. Royall had nothing but praise for her caretaker, who "spoke very good English, and was remarkable well skilled in her business."[15]

Enoch Johnson (perhaps a relative of the proprietor), "a friendly man, but possessed of little general information," operated the ferry crossing on the Chattahoochee River as early as 1828.[16] When James Stuart passed through in 1833, he found Johnson's Tavern still in operation, but thought the place "of a very inferior description," even though it had been recommended by well-to-do John Crowell, the Indian agent. In fact, Stuart deemed it "one of the worst sleeping places I have seen in this country."[17]

Prior to the loss of their Georgia lands and the rise of Columbus, Indians controlled the Chattahoochee River crossings. The most frequent stopping place for travelers heading west from Fort Mitchell was at Uchee Bridge, so called (euphemistically) for the rocky streamed ford at the juncture of Big and Little Uchee Creeks that made for easier passage in high water. One of the largest Lower Creek towns, Uchee (or Yuchi), a thriving settlement comprising nearly one hundred "huts," lay some three miles west on the Federal Road.[18]

The nearby inn, called Uchee Stand or Bridge, seems to have opened in 1820, shortly after the Creek Indian factory at Fort Mitchell closed. Adam

Basil Hall's sketch, *Indian Huts West of the Chatahoochie River 1 Apl 1828.* Courtesy of the Lilly Library, Indiana University, Bloomington, Indiana.

Hodgson described it as a windowless "log building of one story in the yard, with three beds."[19] The inn and a store were operated by Thomas Anthony of Philadelphia and owned by Colonel George Lovett, a wealthy Creek chief whose father, James Lovett, had been a trader. The son served as an official Creek interpreter and earned his military title in the Creek War, serving alongside William McIntosh and the National Creek forces who fought the Red Sticks.[20] Haynes Crabtree acquired the tavern within a few years.[21] Lukas Vischer, a traveler from Switzerland, passed through in 1824 and found that "one may fare none too badly and drink especially good coffee" at Crabtree's.[22]

The Marquis de Lafayette spent the night there, too. General Lafayette's secretary was impressed by the inn's situation and declared his visit to the nearby Indian village "one of the most delightful sojourns that I have experienced."[23]

Lukas Vischer's 1824 sketch of George Lovett's daughter-in-law. Courtesy of the Vischer family.

Between Tyrone Power's "Sodom" on the Chattahoochee and Montgomery, early travelers encountered a variety of accommodations. For a brief time immediately following the Creek War many of the proprietors were Indians, although they soon sold their holdings outright or took on white partners. Since travel after nightfall was both impractical and dangerous, entrepreneurs established stage stops or stands approximately a day's ride from each other. The first generation of stage stops were spaced fourteen to sixteen miles apart along the road. As regularly scheduled stage routes proliferated in the late 1820s and 1830s, the average distance traveled daily increased, as did the desire of travelers to avoid stops and cover distances faster.

Consequently, growing numbers of travelers found themselves trudging down the Federal Road at night. The next stop to the west after Uchee Bridge was Royston's Inn, operated from 1825 to 1836. The area would later be noted for the abandoned earthwork known as "Sand Fort," thrown up by General Thomas Jesup's army in the Second Creek War. James Stuart found this to be "a very tolerable country inn."[24] Prior to 1825, Thomas Carr and his Creek wife evidently ran the inn. When the petulant Lukas Vischer stopped in March 1824, he found "a miserable room . . . [with] miserable beds. Two mirrors and a clock were supposed to decorate the wall, which was however covered with dust, and it seems that no one here knows anything about winding a clock."[25]

Westbound travelers next came to Lewis's Tavern, near the site of abandoned Fort Bainbridge (modern Hurtsboro), an establishment operated by Kendall Lewis and his wife, daughter of the leading Creek chief Big Warrior.[26] Lewis was, according to his friend Thomas S. Woodward, "as perfect a gentleman, in principle, as ever lived in or out of the nation, and had plenty, and it in fine style."[27] Bernhard declared Lewis's Tavern "a handsome house, the best that we had found in the Indian territory."[28] Moreover, the food prepared by Lewis's Creek wife was "excellent."[29]

By the time Stuart arrived in 1833, the inn had become Harris's Hotel, a place with amenities as well as incongruities. While no doubt relieved to have secured "a single-bedded room," Stuart was "surprised to find Cowper's poems on the table in the room, while there was not even a pane of glass in the window." He also rated a towel and basin for his own use, while fellow travelers made do with a communal water basin and a single "very large towel . . . hung on a wooden roller, fixed to the side of the wall."[30]

A day's ride would deliver the traveler to Big Warrior's.[31] When William S. Potts visited in 1828, Big Warrior's son, Jargee, and daughters-in-law were keeping the stand. Potts declared two of Jargee's wives, the only Creeks there the day he visited, "modest, handsome women."[32] Bernhard, Duke of Saxe-Weimar-Eisenach, observed at Big Warrior's Tavern that a journey's tedium could be relieved by amusements such as card playing and horseracing, although, ever the critic, he noted the "middling unsightly" appearance of the local horses.[33]

Following removal of the Creeks from this last portion of their homeland in the 1830s, Americans moved in and, at the midpoint of the road between Columbus and Montgomery, established the new town of Tuskegee. Several inns immediately arose, including one hailed by Buckingham as "one of the neatest and cleanest we had seen in the South; and though very humble in its appearance and furniture, there was such an air of neatness, cleanliness, and order about it, that it excited our warm commendation."[34] This was perhaps William Dent's hotel, visited by Dr. Motte in 1836, who noted the presence of "rival" hotels in the newly established town.[35]

Lucas Tavern in Waugh, Alabama, located on the Old Federal Road. Photograph by Alex L. Bush, 1950s. Courtesy of the Alabama Department of Archives and History.

The freshness of the Tuskegee inns stood in stark contrast to Walker's Tavern at Pole Cat Springs, twelve miles to the west, the site of Buckingham's undeniably worst night on the Federal Road. As rain poured through the roof, he lay sleepless, tossing and turning, listening to the nocturnal sounds of his fellow travelers through the inn's thin walls.[36]

Mrs. Lucas ran what was no doubt the most celebrated tavern on the Federal Road, and the sole example still standing. Stuart described her as once "a good-looking woman, but now . . . fatter at her age, (only thirty-five) than any woman I ever saw. She is married now for the second time, her first husband having been killed in a conflict with the Indians. She takes the entire management of her house, and from what I saw and heard, manages it admirably."[37]

As the town of Montgomery developed, accommodations of various sorts arose to meet the needs of river and road travelers. By 1839, James Buckingham found "excellent quarters in the best hotel we had seen since leaving New York."[38] From Montgomery, many travelers opted to travel on to Mobile by

Tavern and stage stop at Fort Dale, Butler County, Alabama, built around 1840 to replace the original inn called "The Palings." Photographed by W. N. Manning in 1935, at that time a tenant residence. Courtesy of the Historic American Buildings Survey, Library of Congress.

steamboat, and consequently there were few stage stops and inns along the
southern stretch of the Federal Road. A standout among accommodations in
this area was "The Palings." The name referred to the nearby wooden palisade
of Fort Dale, a militia post erected during the Creek raids of 1818–19. Travelers
stayed at "The Palings," the "flourishing plantation" of Colonel Sam Dale, who
was, according to Adam Hodgson, "an intelligent man; and among his books
I saw the Bible, the Koran, a hymn book, Nicholson's Encyclopedia, Sterne,
Burns, Cowper, Coelebs, Camilla, and the Acts of the Alabama Legislature."
Hodgson felt "accommodated tolerably."[39]

Another notable stop was operated by Duncan McMillan and his family
in Monroe County. Established in the 1820s, the inn was nothing more than a
private residence with a small room for boarders.[40]

The town of Claiborne began as a fort and military camp established early
in the Creek War on 150-foot-high Weatherford's Bluff overlooking the Alabama River, previously the location of a plantation and ferry owned by John

Loading Cotton on the Steamboat Magnolia *on the Alabama River.* Engraving from *Ballou's Pictorial Drawing-Room Companion*, May 4, 1861. Courtesy of the Alabama Department of Archives and History.

Weatherford, a wealthy Creek and brother of William Weatherford. The town grew rapidly after the war and by 1820 was a thriving place of two thousand residents. With a fine deep river anchorage and a ferry crossing for an important branch of the Federal Road, Claiborne became a major connector between Alabama's developing water and land communication systems. For a time, in the 1820s and 1830s, the amount of postage accrued at Claiborne ranked second only to Mobile in southwest Alabama.[41] As a major cotton port, Claiborne's wealth and prosperity made it a compelling destination for overland travelers well into the 1830s, as exemplified by General Lafayette's visit there in 1825.[42]

Judge Thomas Stocks of Georgia penned one of the earliest accounts of Claiborne's inns on his tour of newly ceded lands after the Creek War. Arriving on May 3, 1819, he "spent the night at Shearleys Tavern. Where I [w]as bit so bad by gnats and chinces [bed bugs] etc. that in the morning I changed my lodging by going to Mr. Maburys where I was some better off but still badly accommodated."[43]

By the time Hamilton visited Claiborne in 1831, he found a stagnant town. A similar fate befell Blakeley, near the south end of the Federal Road, which briefly rivaled Mobile in population and economic vitality. In 1820, when

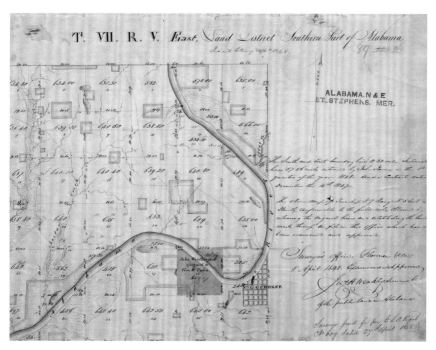

Original survey showing the township of Claiborne on the Alabama River. Courtesy of the Bureau of Land Management, General Land Office.

Adam Hodgson passed through, he saw not only a "fine range of warehouses" for the cotton market but also "the stumps of the trees which had been felled to make room for this young city still standing in the streets."[44] Both towns boomed with the cotton economy, as the famous chute at Weatherford's Bluff testified, but neither outlasted the reign of King Cotton. Both had become ghost towns by the end of the Civil War, with most of their finer structures dismantled and moved to adjacent communities.

Venison and corn, traditional Indian foods, were staples on travelers' plates at inns, taverns, and campsites along the road—as Adam Hodgson said, "plain substantial fare."[45] The harshest critics, like Thomas Hamilton, traveling in April 1831, might complain of venison that ranged from "tolerable" to "rancid," but most accepted meals with little complaint, and occasionally with enthusiasm.[46] Travelers experienced an eclectic mix of meats and vegetables along the Federal Road that had, by the early nineteenth century, come to define not simply "Indian" food, but "southern" food as well. Venison, turkey, and corn, usually in the form of fried "corn cakes" or cornbread, were ubiquitous.

Cast iron skillet, recovered from Fort Stoddert. Courtesy of Brent McWilliams.

On the tavern table, bacon, eggs, roasted chickens, cream, and butter testified to the prominence of domesticated hogs, chickens, and dairy cattle in the region. Introduced in the eighteenth century and adopted readily by Creek in-laws of colonial deerskin traders eager for tastes of home, these animals transformed not only Creek foodways but also the very environment of the Southeast. Cattle and pigs, in particular, decimated river bottom canebrakes, and, like chickens (called by the Indians "dung heap fowl") brought animal litter and filth into the heart of Indian settlements. Pigs ranged freely in forests, feeding off acorns, hickory nuts, and other mast, and both pigs and chickens consumed waste around homes, including those operating as taverns.

Prepared and served by Indian women and enslaved Africans, this new southern food represented a true fusion of ingredients, cuisines, and serving styles. William S. Potts in 1828 observed the manner in which the inventive Creek women at Big Warrior's Stand turned age-old techniques to new

Dutch oven recovered from the site of Fort Claiborne. Courtesy of the Alabama Department of Archives and History.

purposes by preparing coffee using traditional mortar, pestle, and sifter: "the coffee was poured into a hollowed stump, and beat with a stick of wood until mashed up, when it was sifted into a basket." Potts judged the coffee "thick," the women's ham and chicken dishes "bad," and their cornbread "very sour." This last was *Tuk-like-tokse*, in the Muscogee language of the Creeks, made from fermented corn dough. Most travelers would no doubt have agreed with Potts; the distinctive tang of sour cornbread and the more famous *sofkee*, a gruel made from hominy soaked in wood ash lye, were acquired tastes.[47]

The first of the Federal Road's tavern keepers and landlords, particularly in the 1820s and 1830s, made immense profits, no matter how dissatisfied their customers. For as Hodgson observed, in the absence of real competition, "the necessities of the traveller, compel him to submit to any arbitrary charge."[48] As travel increased and taverns proliferated, quite naturally the quality of service and food improved. Many later travelers complimented tavern meals served amply and, on occasion, with style and flair. Like many others, the Duke of

Imported British and locally made Indian ceramics recovered at the site of Moniac's house on the Federal Road: (a) green edge-decorated pearlware plate rim; (b) saucer rim with hand-painted brown band; (c–g) plain pearlware body sherds; (h) plain fine sand tempered sherd, probably historic Creek Indian pottery. Courtesy Center for Archaeological Studies, University of South Alabama.

Saxe-Weimar-Eisenach declared Lewis Tavern meals "the best."[49] Likewise, Lucas Tavern earned accolades from James Stuart. His remarkable meal of

> chicken-pie, ham, vegetables, pudding, and pie, was so neatly put upon the table, and so well cooked,—and the dessert, consisting of dried fruits, preserved strawberries and plumbs, was so excellent of all its kinds, and withal the guests seemd to be made so welcome to every thing that was best. . . . The preserved plum was in as great perfection here as at Ferrybridge. There was wine on the table, as well as brandy and water; and plenty of time was allowed us to partake of our repast. The whole charge was only three-quarters of a dollar for each person. This certainly was as comfortable a meal as we found anywhere in travelling in the United States.[50]

Emigrants, in marked contrast to wealthier tourists and business travelers, camped out and prepared their own meals. Harriet Martineau jotted down her impressions of a typical emigrant campsite: a "fire would be blazing, the pot boiling, the shadowy horses behind, at rest . . . [campers] stretching their sail-cloth on poles to windward, or drawing up the carts in line, or gathering sticks, or cooking."[51] As the rush to acquire former Indian lands accelerated in the

1830s, Tyrone Power found the Federal Road "covered" with families heading west.[52] Those forced by economics to bypass the ostensible comfort of a tavern meal and hired bed still needed to purchase provisions, such as corn and fodder for horses and oxen. Adam Hodgson berated tavern keepers for selling such essentials, procured cheaply from Indians, at double the price to travelers. As Alabama Fever spread, many such entrepreneurs made "a rapid fortune."[53]

SIX

THE CHANGING PHYSICAL AND CULTURAL LANDSCAPE

Sensory experiences of the southern landscape had profound impacts on travelers of the Federal Road. The power of violent and unpredictable storms, the hazards of night travel, the raw and rugged terrain, and encounters with native peoples at ease in these settings both frightened and fascinated visitors.

Experiencing such ordeals, titillating dangers, and novel scenes inspired many travelers to pen "picturesque" vignettes that count among the richest literary accounts of early Alabama. They reveal both the natural beauty of premodern Alabama and the emotional reactions aroused by travelers' encounters with an unspoiled landscape and its colorful inhabitants.[1]

Many travelers did find the region an enchanting wilderness of mesmerizing visual tableaus. Night brought the "moving lights" of fireflies that "delighted with their beauty, evanescent as it was."[2] The observant might marvel during the day at "tassels of black butterflies hanging from the extremities of the twigs" of blooming sourwood.[3] Travelers also found the sonic landscape compelling, whether their "ears were stunned with the frog concerts" or the "crash of near thunder."[4] As Thomas Hamilton and his fellow passengers walked through the night forest, he thought nothing "could be more beautiful than the scene presented by the forest. The glare of our torches, as we continued slowly advancing amid the darkness; the fires of the Indian encampments seen at a distance through the trees, and the wild figures by which they were surrounded; the multitude of fire-flies which flickered everywhere among the foliage,—formed a combination of objects which more than compensated in picturesque beauty, for all the difficulties we had yet encountered."[5] More than one traveler commented on the "charming groves of magnolia, holly, rhododendron, &c."[6]

Honeysuckle. Courtesy Kathryn Braund.

Women travelers most frequently noticed the native wildflowers. During her 1830 spring ride to Montgomery, Anne Royall reported, "the whole southern country is one garden of flowers . . . [that] grow close to the ground; they are a species of pink, or bright scarled [scarlet] red, precisely like the garden pink, and so thick on the ground, that it appears to be covered with red satin. These are again over-topped with white, purple and blue flowers, none of which I had ever seen before. These were on the dry or upland, and fairly illuminated the woods." Along streams, she spotted "*woodbine*," which she described as "something like jessamine, and produces a most brilliant flower."[7] Harriet Martineau, generally so dour in her observations of the South, expressed delight on her travels through the Creek Nation in 1835 at finding the woods "superb in their spring beauty. The thickets were in full leaf; and the ground was gay with violets, may-apple, buck-eye, blue lupin, iris, and crow-poison. The last is like the white lily, growing close to the ground." She felt awe for "the grandest flower of all, perhaps the most exquisite I ever beheld . . . the honeysuckle of the southern woods."[8] She described it as "a globe of blossoms, larger than my hand . . . with the richest and most harmonious colouring, the most delicate long anthers, and the flowers exquisitely grouped among the leaves." This was, she declared, "the queen of flowers."⁹

Counterpoised with such scenes of natural beauty were not infrequent scenes of natural devastation. In 1820 near Blakeley, Adam Hodgson encountered evidence of a tornado or hurricane, "one of the most sublimely dreadful spectacles I ever beheld. Thousands of large pine trees lay torn and shattered on each other, only one in four or five having been left standing . . . ravages of which extended nearly twelve miles. Some had been thrown down with such prodigious violence, that their thick trunks were broken into two or three pieces by the fall; others were splintered from the top nearly to the bottom; while others were lying on each other four or five thick, their branches intertwined as if they had been torn up by the roots in a body."¹⁰

There were many natural curiosities. George Featherstonhaugh encountered the "stuffed skins of three extraordinarily thick *Diamond rattlesnakes*" on the porch of Mr. Cook's tavern. One of them, nearly eight feet in length and over thirteen inches in diameter, more than impressed the Englishman.¹¹ Stuffed panthers, bearskins, and other natural curiosities also drew appreciative comments from visitors to stage stops where such trophies were displayed.¹² However, few travelers actually saw the more threatening natural predators— alligators, panthers, and bears—alive on the much-frequented road.

Although travelers' impressions of the landscape ranged from hellish wilderness to wild, primal beauty, most writers recognized the changes occurring as settlers poured into the state of Alabama. Charles Lyell, on his second visit in 1846, stopped to inspect trees felled for cotton fields. Growth rings of trees, cut generally two to three feet from the ground, revealed a forest of centenarians with 120 to 320 years of growth. Sadly, the traveler noted, "no such trees will be seen by posterity," as he mused on "how many years it would take to restore such a forest if once destroyed." Such massive forest clearing resulted in deepening erosional gullies and silt-choked rivers, an ecological nightmare. Regarding the rapid growth of Columbus, Georgia, and the cotton mills springing up along the Chattahoochee River, Lyell noted, "a large proportion of the fish, formerly so abundant, . . . have been stifled by the mud."¹³ His impression came a week after the last detachment of Creek Indians left Columbus, forcibly deported to Indian Territory.¹⁴

Modern readers might assume that the cramped carriages and inns travelers endured would leave them longing for solitude. On the contrary, the vast wilderness frequently left travelers forlorn with almost overwhelming feelings of isolation. After riding miles along the Federal Road in 1832 and seeing

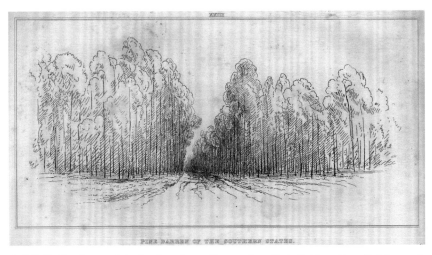

Basil Hall's *Pine Barren of the Southern States*. Plate 23 from *Forty Etchings: From Sketches made with Camera Lucida in 1827 and 1828* by Captain Basil Hall. "A considerable portion of the Southern States of America, and even as far as North Carolina, is covered with boundless forests of pine-trees. These districts are called Pine Barrens, and the soil being generally sandy, with a scanty supply of water, they are probably destined to remain forever in the state of a useless wilderness. Upwards of five hundred miles of our journey lay through these desolate forests, and I have therefore thought it worthwhile to give a Sketch, which is sufficiently characteristic of these singular regions." Courtesy of the Alabama Department of Archives and History.

"neither habitation nor an inhabitant to disturb the solitude and majesty of the wilderness," a melancholy John Howard Payne confided to a friend that he could not adequately express his feelings.[15] As Adam Hodgson traversed "a most solitary pine barren, on a high ridge" in the southern stretch of the road in 1820, he spotted "a fingerpost of wood fastened to a tree and pointing down a grass path, and on which was written 'To Pensacola,'" and he suddenly "felt more lonely and more distant from home at that moment, than at any time since I lost sight of my native shores."[16] Even as late as 1839, travelers might proceed "for miles in succession . . . [seeing] neither a human being, a fence, a rood of cleared land, nor anything indeed that could indicate the presence of man, or the trace of civilization." "We felt," wrote James Buckingham in 1839, "the solitude of the woods in all its fulness."[17]

The poet and novelist William Gilmore Simms captured, better than most, the heightened sensory experience of a traveler on the Federal Road, as the natural and cultural milieus combined to render an indelible memory:

stiffened with cold, knee deep in mud and water, and anxious to proceed, in the fear of losing the next stage from Fort Mitchell to Montgomery, I could not help admiring the high degree of picturesque which entered into the scene around me. The shouting of the Indians in self encouragement, and in their quick detached and fragmentary language—the cheerings of our own party—innumerable torches, scattered about the woods, and on the marge of the swollen waters— the rushing of the waters themselves—the neighing and struggling of the horses, up to their middles in the creek swamp—added to the cheerless and wild character of the prospect, and those associations, which sought in vain to reconcile, the present with the past fortunes and labors of the Indian tribes—all combined to give a graphic force to a picture, worthy of the pencil of Rembrandt.[18]

For many travelers, the Indians along the upper part of the Federal Road— from Fort Mitchell to Line Creek—were simply part of the exotic, wild landscape. As traffic increased along the Federal Road after the Creek War, the Creek Indians became both attractions and outfitters for tourists. Indian proprietors established and ran the first taverns and stage stops, and other Creeks established ferries and toll bridges in their country. Toll fees varied. In 1824 Lucas Vischer jotted down the rates: "for a four-wheeled conveyance 50 cents, for a two-wheeled 25 cents, for a rider 12 ½ cents, for a pedestrian 6 ½ cents."[19] Before long, white operators replaced native ones and increasingly Indians were marginalized, as emigrants and travelers found ways to avoid payments at river crossings. Still, Indians remained fixtures along the road as guides, selling produce and souvenirs, performing various menial chores, and working for hire.[20]

In the 1820s and 1830s, encountering Indians on the Federal Road was surely part of the allure for tourists. Auguste Levasseur first sighted Indians at the Creek Agency (near present-day Macon, Georgia) as they dried clothes around a large fire at a house not far from the road. Levasseur likely summed up the attitudes of most foreign travelers: "my attention was very keenly excited by this encounter, the first that I had had of this kind. I had heard so much spoken of the customs of these men of nature, and like all who live in a civilized country, I had formed such singular ideas of them that the least of their gestures, the tiniest piece of their clothing and their armor was nearly as great a cause of astonishment for me as was, in turn, the fact that the Indians appeared to experience nothing at all upon seeing us."[21]

Whenever opportunity presented itself, travelers stopped to visit Indian towns, watch ball play, view children at their games, or simply observe the Creeks in their own communities.[22] Some took pleasure in interacting with those they encountered. Hodgson was "amused by Mukittaw, a fine Indian lad," who interrupted him while he was writing in his journal. Hodgson in

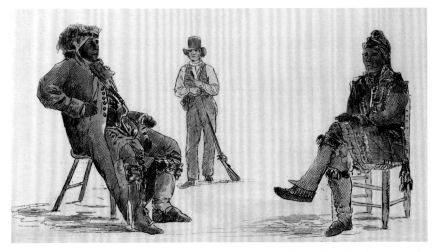

Chiefs of the Creek Nation and a Georgian Squatter. From *Forty Etchings: From Sketches made with Camera Lucida in 1827 and 1828* by Captain Basil Hall. The man on the left is Little Prince, head of the Creek National Council, who died a few weeks after meeting Hall. Courtesy of the Beinecke Rare Book and Manuscript Library, Yale University.

turn amused the boy by allowing him to examine "my little shaving apparatus, and my pocket inkstand."[23] Others listened eagerly to tales of Indian massacres and attacks.[24] Grilling the natives about cultural norms was common. Among the topics travelers of the writing kind thought to report were the multiple wives of Chilly McIntosh, whose plantation was a well-frequented stop near Fort Mitchell in the 1820s, Indian dress and appearance, and activities of every sort.

Seemingly innocent encounters between travelers and Creeks prove quite revealing to modern sensibilities. Bernhard, who found himself hiking four miles to Walker's Tavern after his carriage overturned, came upon Indians going about their normal daily activities and preparing a meal. From them he "bought a species of nuts, which were roasted, groundnuts, and amused myself with the propensity to thievery a young Indian displayed. As I was putting the nuts in my pocket, one or more would drop, instantly the young fellow would step forward, as if by accident, set his foot on the nut, take it between his toes, and move off."[25] In his amusement, Bernhard overlooked the poverty engulfing the Creek people or the few means they had, in their shattered postwar economy, to overcome it.

Playing jokes on fellow travelers was a common occurrence and more than one thought to involve Indians. Playing on the fears of fellow travelers, P. T.

A Choctaw camp near Mobile, by Gritzner, ca. 1850. Such temporary shelters were common through-out Indian country. Courtesy of the Mobile History Museum.

Barnum and Buckingham Smith (both performers) hired Indians to stage mock attacks and chases, paying them for their trouble and enjoying, all the while, the discomfort of their companions.[26]

Anne Royall found the road between Columbus and Montgomery "strewn with Indian camps" in the cooler months, when the Creeks sold corn and venison, as well as "Indian corn-leaves," which served as horse fodder in the absence of hay. These corn shucks, like the lighter wood (resin-rich longleaf pine knots) they sold for travelers' torches, represented the work of women, whose traditional roles involved not only all agricultural production but also collecting firewood.[27] Women fashioned beaded moccasins and finger-woven bandolier bags for sale.[28] And Creek women tended to travelers' needs at inns and taverns as cooks, waitresses, and maids.

The temporary structures and camps that Indians established along the road did not impress visitors. Tyrone Power found their "condition of the majority . . . wretched in the extreme: most of the families were living in wig-wams, built of bark or green boughs, of the frailest and least comfortable con-struction; not an article of furniture except a kettle."[29] Adam Hodgson more accurately described these structures as traditional shelters used at winter hunting camps, but now built near the Federal Road to access the market cre-ated by traveling Americans. These "rude dwellings" consisted "of four upright

Lucas Vischer's watercolor of a Creek Indian hunter, dated
March 15, 1824. Courtesy of the Vischer family.

saplings, and a rough covering of pine-bark, which they strip from the trees
with a neatness and rapidity which we could not imitate." These dignified and
stoic residents made a "very picturesque appearance," according to more than
one traveler.[30]

Communication along the road was challenging. In early 1820, Adam Hodgson and his party searched in vain one night for water for their horses. When
they came on an Indian camp, they were dismayed to find the Creeks they
encountered could not understand them, or, as Hodgson correctly observed,
"we could not make ourselves intelligible." He later took the time to learn a
few Muscogee words.[31] Travelers and Creeks muddled through the morass of
cross-cultural and multilingual exchange in a variety of ways. Most exchanges

DR. MOTTE'S CREEK DICTIONARY

Dr. Jacob Rhett Motte traveled from Columbus to Tuskegee along the Federal Road in 1836 during the Second Creek War. In the course of that war, he claimed to have become "quite proficient in the Creek language," and his published account of the Creek and Seminole wars includes a selection of Muscogee words. According to Motte, some words were "frequently used to express different things; the meaning communicated by the emphasis and tone of voice, which the Indian is capable of the sweetest modulation. Tis music itself to hear the Indians conversing in hours of social intercourse." Many of the words below, selected from his lexicon, clearly relate to travel.[33]

Nouns
Bed—To*pah*
Corn—*Ah*cheh
Cow—*Wau*kah
Fire—*Toot*kah
Horse—Cholocko
Money—Chatta kanah *wah*
Night—Neth-lee
No—Cush
Stars—Koto chumpah
Sun—Netah Hossee

Verbs
Ligico—I ride.
Ligitska—you ride.
Okagen—we ride.
Ligungis—rode.
Ligofen—when I ride.
Aieton—to go.
Aiepus—I go.
Aiungis—I went.
Hateton—to stop.
Hattis cheh—stop.
Nisseton—to sell.

Conversation
Ista na'atitska?—Where do you come from?
Tuskegee n'atiis cheh—I come from Tuskegee.
Ista n'aiatlonistska?—Where are you going?
Where do you live?—Istah ma ehootah cheh?
That's my house—Sacheh sookoo.
Hatchee tabaia—Across the creek.
What's your name?—Nakin *chief* ka *teh*?
I am your friend—An hisseh clittah *mas* cheh.
I want it—Chi-ah-chis-cheh.
Buy it—Nis-us-*cheh*.
Eight of a dollar—Ka-lai-*zu*-cheh.
Quarter of a dollar—Kan-*zat*-kah.

involved "sign language" or "pantomime" although a fair share of the Creeks spoke English. As John Howard Payne searched for the branch road to Tuckabatchee in 1835, he encountered two Creek women and asked them how far they were from their destination. The women "half covered a finger, to express that it was half a mile further, and smiling, added, '*sneezer—much*,' meaning that we should find lots of our brethren, the sneezers, there."[32]

Some Creeks, like Hamley, a young man who met up with General Lafayette's traveling party, spoke "very good English." Hamley, who had been educated in the states, lived in a well-furnished and hospitable house and entertained the traveling Frenchmen by playing Indian tunes on his violin. Levasseur, the general's secretary, thought the house where Hamley lived with his two wives "indicated the presence of a half-civilized man."[34] Today we consider Hamley a prime example of a Creek man who was, like many of his fellow Creeks, creatively adapting to changing times. The French writer added that the young man had "a remarkable stature and beauty." Dressed in the latest Creek fashion, he wore a fringed coat, sported a bandolier bag with "little beads of a thousand colors," and wore a turban fashioned from a brightly colored shawl "elegantly" around his head. He told the visitors he had "escaped" from the American school because he preferred living among his own people. An enemy of William McIntosh, who had just sold the Creeks' Georgia lands to the United States, Hamley was a prudent man who not only continued to hunt but also kept deer penned like livestock near his dwelling when hunts were unproductive. He also housed and protected slaves who had run away from the Americans, and they paid for his "hospitality" by work.[35] His house and living arrangements represented an interesting admixture of traditional Creek values and new adaptations to American culture. Like all Creeks who operated taverns and inns and lived in proximity to the road, he was familiar with American and European cultural practices and outlooks. And, like most other Creeks of mixed ancestry, he fully identified as a Creek and was helping to redefine Creek identity and culture.

The majority of the Creek population lived in towns and on outlying plantations, virtually all at some distance from the Federal Road, Cussita and Tuckabatchee being two important exceptions. Cussita, a large Creek town on the east bank of the Chattahoochee River, was a frequent stopping place for travelers who reached the river. Until its inhabitants were forcibly removed following the cession of their land to Georgia, the town boasted over one hundred homes, gardens, and a traditional hot house, town square, and chunky yard.[36] After 1826, the American town of Columbus grew up near the site.

Travelers along the Federal Road witnessed many of the upheavals and ultimate removal of the Creeks from the southern states. A "work of plunder and corruption" via treaties, a disgusted George Featherstonhaugh called it.[37] The increase in American settlements around them resulted in, as Featherstonhaugh noted, "the total dissolution of order." He observed Indians begging, stealing whiskey, and the rampant drunkenness of many whose lives had been shattered by the loss of their land.[38] After the cession of their Georgia land following the Treaty of Washington in 1826, Lower Creeks attempting to resettle on the Creeks' remaining Alabama lands were, as Basil Hall observed, "wandering about like bees whose hive has been destroyed."[39] With the Creek Nation in political disarray, nothing could curb the actions of unscrupulous white squatters and land speculators, who cheated Indians along the border and, indeed, in their own remaining territory.

More than one traveler witnessed the callous disregard for Indian rights by those who cheated, abused, and insulted them.[40] When talk of Indian Removal came up during dinner at Lewis's Tavern, the Reverend William Potts engaged in a "warm debate" with another traveler "who was disposed to take sides against the Creeks." Potts's sympathies clearly lay with the Creek women, who stoically cooked and served the travelers' meals and endured their insults.[41] A few years later, with forced removal underway, James Buckingham asked an Indian woman if removal was "a blessing." "She made no answer," but he later learned the innkeeper, a "half-blood Indian," was so enraged "when the question was repeated to him, that he was 'perfectly mad,' in the language of our informant, and declared his regret that he had missed the opportunity to shoot me for so saying."[42]

As tensions mounted, incidents between Indians and travelers—and between Indians and trespassing settlers—increased. Tales of robbery and murder, most of them exaggerated, caused P. T. Barnum and his traveling companions to arm themselves with "guns, pistols, bowie-knives, etc."[43] Mounting violence between Creeks and Americans by 1836 escalated into war. In addition to looting white settlements along the Chattahoochee, Creeks enraged over encroachment and abuse by white settlers again focused on the roadways. By May attacks on stage-coaches effectively halted travel through the Creek Nation.[44] Armed Creeks destroyed bridges, burned stages, and killed passengers.[45] In July 1836, one federal officer at an army encampment at Tuskegee reported that:

> Every half mile from Fort Mitchell to Tuskegee, bears heart-rending proofs of their savage and unsparing mode of warfare. The road presents such scenes of

blood shedding and burning as can hardly be conceived. At least nine-tenths of the dwellings and farm houses are consumed, and in some instances, the unfortunate victims to Indian barbarity are mixed up in one pile with the cinders of their former dwellings. On Friday we passed the spot made famous by the attack on four stages; the coaches, horses, and all, must have been burned as they stood. Two wheels only remain, besides the bones of the horses and the iron work of the carriages.[46]

Once the Creek rebellion was quickly contained, the US government used this occasion to accelerate forced removal of all remaining Creeks from the state of Alabama, many by way of the Federal Road. Captured Creek men were marched from Fort Mitchell toward Montgomery under guard of federal troops "handcuffed two together, and a long chain passing between the double file connecting them all together."[47] Among the witnesses to this sorry affair was John James Audubon, who arrived at Fort Mitchell in February 1837 to find one hundred Creek men "confined in Irons." As he proceeded west, he overtook "about two thousand" Creeks being marched toward Montgomery. The scene of "Indians in sorrow," he wrote to friends, "produced on my mind an aflicting series of reflections more powerfuly felt than easy of description—the numerous groups of Warriors, of half clad females and of naked babes, trudging through the mire under the residue of their ever scanty stock of Camp furniture, and household utensiles—The evident regret expressed in the masked countenances of some and the tears of others—the howlings of their numerous dogs; and the cool demeanour of the chiefs,—all formed such a Picture as I hope I never will again witness in reality."[48]

The Federal Road was a conduit that enabled both immigration and deportation on massive scales. The unfortunate reality was simply this: settlers and the enslaved had replaced the indigenous population of the region. Cultural reordering began immediately following the Treaty of Fort Jackson, which ended the Creek War of 1813–14. Rich soils of the Black Belt and river bottomlands acted as magnets for those afflicted with Alabama Fever. By the mid-1830s, travelers could see cotton bales loaded onto steamboats at Montgomery and Claiborne, and "a fine range of warehouses" at Blakeley.[49] As travelers peered from carriages that once passed through seemingly endless forests, they now saw "extensive fields of the richest soil, perfectly cleared of all timber, and even the stumps of the trees rooted up and removed."[50] Like Alex Mackay, who arrived in Montgomery in 1846, they could also see slaves working "on either side of the road; their condition betokening, at a glance, the character of their owner, some being well clad, apparently well fed, and hilarious in

Slave quarters on the Will Crenshaw Plantation, near Greenville, Butler County. Photograph by W. N. Manning, 1935. Courtesy Historic American Building Survey, Library of Congress.

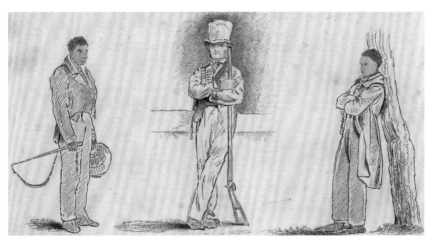

Two Slave Drivers and a Backwoodsman with His Rifle, drawn by Basil Hall using the camera lucida. Plate 20 from Basil Hall's *Forty Etchings*, published in 1829. Courtesy of the Alabama Department of Archives and History.

their dispositions; and others in rags, with their physical frames but poorly supported, and their spirits seemingly much depressed."[51] Harriet Martineau likewise noted the "vacant, unheeding look of the depressed slave."[52] These unwilling immigrants were travelers as well.

Having first walked to new homes in Alabama, many later traveled the road to be resold as chattel property in urban slave marts. By the power of a road, this land had been transformed from Indian territory to the Cotton South. With the removal of Creeks from Alabama in the 1830s, the transformation of the region from Creek country to slave society was complete.[53]

CONCLUDING REFLECTIONS
ON THE FEDERAL ROAD

A road, the dictionary tells us, can be "an open way for vehicles" or "a route or way to an end, conclusion, or circumstance."[1] Roads are conduits or channels or conveyors of people and things. They connect places. They are not normally a destination unto themselves, but rather, a means to an end.

Alabama's Federal Road was not "Federal" for very long. Nor was it much of a road, starting out as a path hacked through the forest, beset by stumps and bogs. And when it began, the Federal Road was not old. Yet the Old Federal Road, as it is widely known, now over two hundred years old, lives on in the hearts and imaginations of modern people.

Much more than a spatial entity, the Old Federal Road is a historical remembrance that connects us to a vanished world. While travelers' tales relay jocular accounts of eccentric characters, bad accommodations, and worse travel conditions, a study of the Old Federal Road reveals a time of cultural mixing and ultimately, great change, whereby a land and its people were remade. The Creek Indians, forced to accommodate American demands for a transportation corridor, rarely prospered from the new opportunities it brought. Instead, the majority of Creeks saw only intrusion, confusion, and the dissolution of order as the road cut an ugly gash through their national sovereignty, much as runoff from hillsides stripped of forest for settlers' fields scoured gullies into their landscape. Ultimately, their land was taken from them. In one of the great ironies of Alabama history, the Federal Road they had long opposed served as the path along which many Creek Indians marched, in chains and under guard, from their homeland to boats that would carry them west of the Mississippi River.

With the removal of the Indians, the changing needs of travelers, and improvements in roadbuilding technology, the original Federal Road quickly

The Creek Indian by Frederic Remington. The painting appeared on the cover of the December 12, 1903, issue of *Collier's Magazine*.

morphed into a network with countless branches. New destinations proliferated and changed the character of the road. As steamboats and railroads gained preeminence in turn, the old road languished, relegated to local traffic. No longer a long-haul route for mail, parcels, troops, settlers, and travelers, a highway that once served national interests faded into a mesh of roads knitting together the state of Alabama, its former importance lost to all but memory.

Today, there are few marked segments of the Old Federal Road. In some places, the road lies beneath modern highways and development; elsewhere, the road is abandoned. Yet visible remnants survive, and modern travelers can visit destinations along the route that shaped not only the road but also the region's history. The power of the road to capture memory is not a recent phenomenon. From the beginning, the exotic and romantic, mixed with gritty reality and danger, left indelible impressions on those who traveled the Federal Road. A road that, like the thousands who traveled it, enchants us still.

The Old Federal Road, early twenty-first century, still beckons to travelers. Courtesy of Mark Dauber.

Tyrone Power's 1834 account of crossing a bridge one stormy night.

Let the reader imagine a figure dressed in a deep yellow shirt reaching barely to the knees, the legs naked; a belt of scarlet wampum about the loins, and a crimson and a dark-blue shawl twisted turban-fashion round of the head; with locks of black coarse hair streaming from under this, and falling loose over the neck or face: fancy one half of such a figure lighted up by a very strong blaze, marking the nimble tread, the swart cold features, sparkling eye, and outstretched muscular arms of the red-man,—the other half, meantime, being in the blackest possible shadow: whilst following close behind, just perceptible through the wreaths of thick smoke, moved the heads of the leading horses; and, over all, flashed at frequent intervals red vivid lightning; one moment breaking forth in a wide sheet, as through an overcharged cloud had burst at once asunder; the next, descending in zigzag lines, or darting through amongst the tall pines and cypress trees; whilst the quick patter of the horses' hoofs were for a time heard loudly rattling over the loose hollow planks, and then again drowned wholly by the crash of near thunder.

Never in my life have I looked upon a scene which holds so vivid a place within my memory: the savage solitude of the jungle, the violence of the storm together with pictorial accessories by which the whole picture was kept in movement, fixed the attention, and can never, I think, be forgotten by those who witnessed it.

—**Tyrone Power,** *Impressions of America during the Years 1833, 1834, and 1835,* 2 vols. (London: Richard Bentley, 1836), 2:88–89.

II

1 TOURING THE OLD FEDERAL ROAD IN ALABAMA

INTRODUCTION

A Modern Traveler's Guide to the Old Federal Road in Alabama

Alabama's present-day transportation network is vastly changed from the historic Indian paths and Federal Road of the early nineteenth century. That our modern roads coincide at all with the region's earliest wagon and postal route testifies to the deep imprint left on Alabama's landscape by the Federal Road. Over the years, substantial sections of the old road fell out of use altogether or were relegated to farm lanes as newer, more useful branches grew from the main trunk. Almost from the beginning, the road shifted and evolved to better accommodate the terrain and to connect with new destinations as American settlements spread across the land. Those of us who attempt today to locate "the" Old Federal Road are confronted with a labyrinth of connecting roads and alternate branches. Anyone intent on driving the Old Federal Road today must necessarily choose one of several possible paths through this maze, each with unavoidable divergences from the original 1811 route.

Moreover, subsequent road construction and maintenance have forever altered the appearance of those sections of the Old Federal Road still in use, now almost unrecognizable as an ancient pathway due to mechanical grading, widening, and straightening to meet modern highway standards. And, of course, these sections are largely paved, an improvement that early nineteenth-century travelers could scarcely have imagined possible.

Despite two centuries of accumulated changes, substantial sections of the old route do remain in use. Enough survives for us to follow paths taken by writers like William Bartram, Peggy Dow, and Benjamin Hawkins, who left us vivid accounts of their ordeals on the Old Federal Road. And we can shadow the thousands of lesser-known travelers—natives as well as newcomers—whose modern descendants can thereby gain a sense of their ancestors' lost world. By retracing this well-worn path that cuts across both space and time,

Abandoned section of the Old Federal Road on private property, showing evidence of compaction and erosion. Courtesy of Mark Dauber.

we can experience the profound truth of poet Jack Kerouac's observation that "the road is life." Whether our motivations are philosophical or genealogical, prompted by a personal journey of self-discovery or simple wanderlust, every modern traveler can enjoy the scenic countryside and visit nature preserves, museums, and historic sites evocative of early America.

We (the authors) have used a variety of archaeological and historical techniques to document the major thoroughfare generally used during the mid-1820s and in many places still in use or only recently abandoned. The driving routes suggested here follow, in large measure, this historic path. Roughly 40 percent of the original Federal Road now crosses private lands, so our driving routes necessarily parallel those stretches of the old route. We have highlighted points of interest that are easily accessed and provide some level of public interpretation. Privately owned segments of the Old Federal Road are, of course, off limits to the public, and travelers are urged to observe landowner rights.

Our guide covers only the Alabama portion of the Old Federal Road. Modern travelers who wish to retrace the roughly 150-mile section in Georgia, between Milledgeville and the Chattahoochee River, are presently left to their own devices. However, we hope this book will inspire development of a similar traveler's guide to that part of the Old Federal Road in our neighboring state. We opted to start our guide to the Old Federal Road at the Chattahoochee River crossing on the Georgia border. While we recognize that the Old Federal Road, like nearly all roads, runs in two directions—and starting at the southern terminus near Mobile, rather than in the middle of the original road, has its own compelling logic—our organizational decision was prompted by the general direction of travel on the Old Federal Road in the 1820s, which by and large ran from northeast to southwest. Many of our historic road chroniclers followed this route in their travels, and readers may wish to refer to their published accounts, some of which are reviewed in the first part of this book.

This guide divides the Old Federal Road into three segments: Eastern, Central, and Southern. Each is slightly different in character, reflecting not only geography but also historic development. Each segment can be enjoyed piecemeal, with numerous opportunities for day trips, or each can serve as an entree to the surrounding areas for extended journeys of exploration. Please note that not all sites have active interpretation. Where appropriate, street address or other location, hours of operation, and contact information are provided. Travelers should confirm this information before visiting. Locations in bold appear on the accompanying tour maps.

For additional information, visit the Old Federal Road website, designed as an accompaniment to this guide, at http://oldfederalroad.info. The site contains additional information, maps, photographs, and links to original travel accounts.

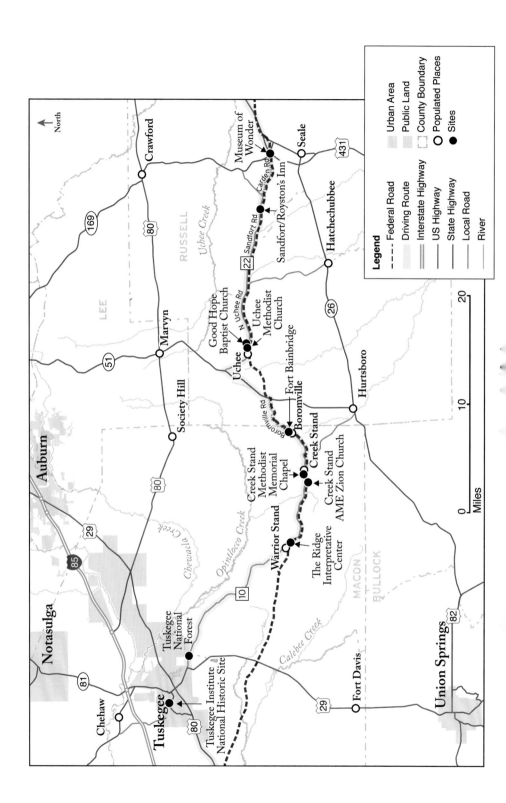

SECTION ONE

Eastern Segment

The Old Federal Road crossed the Chattahoochee River, entering Alabama near Fort Mitchell, and stretched westward to Line Creek, the boundary between the Creek Nation and American territory established by the Treaty of Fort Jackson at the end of the Creek War. For the most part, this stretch of the Old Federal Road still exists today in Macon and Russell Counties, either as a base for modern roads or as a discernible path on private properties (not publicly accessible). It is possible for modern drivers to trace much of the old route along public access dirt and paved roads.

Driving Tour: Fort Mitchell to Tuskegee (Uchee to Warrior Stand)

From Fort Mitchell Heading West. The Federal Road crossed the Chattahoochee near **Fort Mitchell**. Unfortunately, the segment of the road leading west from the fort has been abandoned and is inaccessible for slightly more than five miles. Modern drivers can pick up the road near the junction of AL-169 and US-431. Drivers are cautioned that portions of this route are unpaved. Turn onto AL-169 heading north and almost immediately turn left onto Carden Road (CR-31), an unpaved road; proceed to the junction of Sandfort Road (CR-22), approximately 2.7 miles, and turn left onto CR-22, which is paved.

Sandfort Road (CR-22) follows the Old Federal Road with few deviations. Proceed along CR-22 (Sandfort Road) for 7.5 miles.

Turn right at the intersection with North Uchee Road to remain on CR-22. Continue east for 4.5 miles, passing **Uchee Chapel Methodist Church** and **Good Hope Baptist Church**.

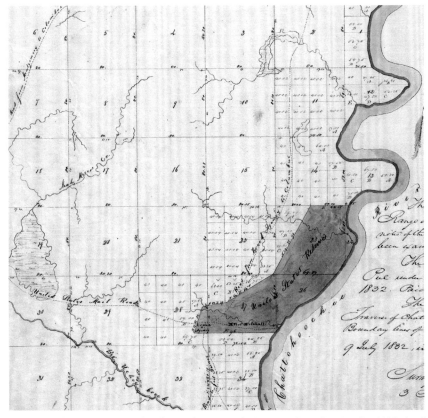

James Weakley's 1834 survey plat of Township 16 North, Range 30 East, showing the Old Federal Road labeled as "United States Mail Road." Courtesy of the Bureau of Land Management, General Land Office.

Turn left onto AL-51S and travel 3.5 miles toward Boromville. Turn right onto Boromville Road (dirt) and continue 5.5 miles to CR-10. Near **Boromville**, you will pass the unmarked site of Fort Bainbridge. Here, the unpaved Boromville Road merges with Sand Road (paved). Turn right onto the pavement and proceed approximately 0.7 of a mile to the junction with Lower Boromville Road. At the junction, Boromville Road veers to the right and returns to an unpaved route. Continue on Boromville Road (dirt) to follow the Old Federal Road. Turn right onto CR-10 at Creek Stand. Proceed west approximately 5.5 miles to **Warrior Stand**.

This route is approximately 30 miles and, aside from the deviation at AL-51, closely parallels the Old Federal Road. At Warrior Stand, the original route

Modern longhorn cattle in Macon County, reminiscent of the type of cattle early travelers would have seen. Courtesy of Raven Christopher.

heads northwest across private property until it reemerges on US-80 near Shorter. To continue the driving tour into the central segment, remain on CR-10 for 10.5 miles, then turn left onto Old Columbus Way/US-29 to Tuskegee.

From Tuskegee, Macon County, Heading East toward Fort Mitchell. Beginning in Tuskegee at the intersection of US-80 and US-29, head south on US-29 for about 1.5 miles, then make a slight left onto Old Columbus Road. In 0.5 of a mile, turn right at County Road 10. Continue along CR-10 for approximately 15.5 miles, passing the old towns of **Warrior Stand** and **Creek Stand**.

Turn left on Boromville Road and proceed for approximately 5.5 miles, passing near the site of **Fort Bainbridge**, to the junction with AL-51. Note that between Lower Boromville Road and Sand Lane, Boromville Road is paved. At the junction with Sand Lane, keep left to remain on Boromville Road, which reverts to an unpaved road. At AL-51, turn left and proceed approximately 3.5 miles north along AL-51 to CR-22 (North Uchee Road). Follow CR-22 for 11.5 miles and then turn right off CR-22 onto Carden Road (CR-31), an unpaved road, and proceed approximately 2.7 miles to AL-169.

Carden Road. Courtesy of Raven Christopher.

Sites and Places to Visit

Phenix City Riverwalk. A paved walkway extends over a mile along the Chattahoochee River, providing views of a whitewater recreational course for hikers, bicyclists, and wildlife observers. There are multiple access points to the park, which extends from Dillingham Street Bridge at the Phenix City Amphitheater (main entrance) to the Fourteenth Street Bridge. The walk is connected by two historic bridges to the Columbus, Georgia, 15-mile river walk on the east side of the Chattahoochee. Open sunrise to sunset.

Fort Mitchell National Historic Site. Now a National Historic Landmark, a fort was built by General John Floyd of Georgia in late 1813 as a supply base for Georgia incursions into hostile Red Stick Creek territory. Named for Georgia Governor David B. Mitchell, the fort remained in operation through the First Seminole War, was rebuilt in 1825, and served as a military post through the Second Seminole and Second Creek Wars. This was John Crowell's base as federal agent to the Creek Nation and the location of his brother's tavern. The circa 1813 fort has been reconstructed adjacent to a National Cemetery. In addition to the fort and tavern, there is a historic cabin and a Visitor Center. Located 10 miles south of Phenix City, Alabama, on AL-165. Open Monday through Saturday, 10:00 A.M. to 5:00 P.M. and Sunday afternoon. There is an admission fee.

Fort Mitchell National Historic Site. Courtesy of Raven Christopher.

Fort Mitchell Military Cemetery. The original graveyard for the US military post is today remembered with a historic marker and several headstones for the people known or believed to have been buried at the fort, including Timpoochee Barnard, a noted Creek headman. Located inside Fort Mitchell Park.

Crowell Family Cemetery. US Indian agent John Crowell and members of the Cantey family are buried in a historic plot inside Fort Mitchell Park, next to Fort Mitchell National Cemetery.

Chattahoochee Indian Heritage Center, Fort Mitchell. Adjacent to Fort Mitchell, the center commemorates Creek inhabitants of the region and the location of an internment camp for Creek Indians forcibly removed from Alabama in the mid-1830s. Notable features include a ceremonial flame sculpture, interpretative panels, and historic markers. The center is entered through Fort Mitchell Historic Site. Open Thursday through Saturday, 10:00 A.M. to 5:00 P.M. and Sunday afternoon.

Asbury School and Mission Historic Marker. Located at the Crowell Family Cemetery, commemorates the Methodist mission school built in 1821 north of Fort Mitchell for Creek Indian students.

Museum of Wonder. Created by local artist Butch Anthony, the museum is open by appointment only and includes a variety of art, found objects, and curiosities ranging from arrowheads to a two-headed duck, "mostly from Alabama." A more accessible drive-through museum of oddities, known as "The World's First Drive Thru Museum," constructed from shipping containers, is located at the intersection of US-431 and AL-169 in Seale and recalls the curiosities that greeted historic travelers along the Old Federal Road. Information about Anthony's museums can be found at http://www.museumofwonder.com.

Eufaula National Wildlife Refuge. The US Fish and Wildlife Service manages this extensive natural resource of nearly 12,000 acres spanning the Chattahoochee River, on the Georgia-Alabama border. In addition to fishing on Walter F. George Lake, visitors to the refuge can view indigenous wildlife in wetland and upland forest habitats. The refuge is noted for overwintering migratory birds and hosts a variety of animal life year-round. In addition to a walking trail, there is a driving (auto and bike) route with observation platforms and towers. The refuge allows visitors to recapture a sense of the historic landscape. The refuge office is located at 367 AL-165, off US-431, 7 miles north of Eufaula, and is open Monday through Friday 8:00 A.M. to 4:30 P.M. CST. Call 334-687-4064 for more information.

Fort Bainbridge and Lewis's Tavern, Boromville. Modern Boromville's modest appearance belies its earlier importance as the site of **Fort Bainbridge** and,

Lewis's Tavern, as envisioned by a modern artist. Courtesy of the Alabama Department of Archives and History.

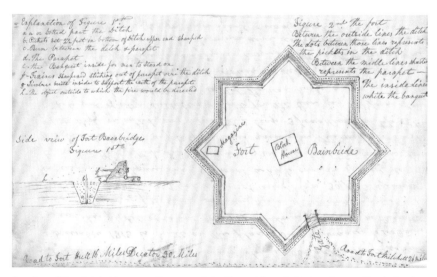

Drawing of Fort Bainbridge, 1814. Courtesy of the General Joseph Graham Papers, North Carolina Department of Archives and History.

later, Lewis's Tavern. As the Creek War was winding down in March 1814, General Joseph Graham's North Carolina militia constructed Fort Bainbridge, the last of the Creek War forts built along the Federal Road, on the ridge dividing the Chattahoochee and Tallapoosa watersheds. The large earthen fort served mainly to guard the US Army's supply route into the Creek Nation. Following the war, Kendall Lewis built a tavern on the abandoned fort site. A number of travelers mentioned Lewis's Tavern in their published accounts. As travel patterns shifted after Indian Removal, new landowners established a plantation here that used extensive slave labor. Modern agricultural practices have erased traces of the fort.

Uchee Chapel Methodist Church. Courtesy of Kathryn Braund.

Uchee Chapel Methodist Church. This building dates to 1859, although the congregation formed in 1836 and was originally housed in a log structure. The present church, a Greek Revival–style building with a temple front, was added to the National Register of Historic Places in 1997. It is located at 5885 North Uchee Road (CR-22).

Good Hope Baptist Church. This historic building, erected in 1857, is not open to the public. Located at 6054 North Uchee Road (CR-22).

Warrior Stand and Creek Stand. Both of these towns began as "stands," taverns situated along the Federal Road. Big Warrior, Speaker for the Creek National Council, owned and operated Warrior Stand in the decade after the Creek War. Creek Stand was run by Tustunnuggee Hopoie, the Little Prince, headman of Coweta and Speaker for the Lower Creeks. Descriptions of these early taverns do not survive. Following Indian Removal, the small agricultural settlements that grew up around them retained these names, memorializing their earlier importance to travelers.

Creek Stand Methodist Memorial Chapel and Historic Cemetery, Creek Stand. The history of the church and its congregation is integral to the Creek Stand settlement. Mount Zion church was established by Alabama Fever settlers, many of whom lay at rest in the cemetery, which was added to the Alabama Historic Cemetery Register in 2016. A replica of the church, the memorial chapel, was constructed with material from the original building. It is not open for public visitation, but the site and historic marker are visible from the road. The publicly accessible cemetery is located off CR-10, 0.2 of a mile east of the junction with CR-79.

Creek Stand A.M.E. Zion Church and Historic Cemetery, Creek Stand. The original church, founded in 1895 by freedmen, stood at the center of the African American Creek Stand community. The cemetery was added to the National Register of Historic Places in 2016 for its significance to Ethnic Heritage and Black Social History. The present church building, erected in 1995, is not open to the public, but visitors can walk through the cemetery, which is the resting place for several subjects of the infamous Tuskegee syphilis study conducted by the US Public Health Service. The site is located on Slim Road, which runs off CR-10 at Creek Stand.

The Ridge Interpretive Center, Warrior Stand. The center features documentary and archaeological findings, in both permanent and temporary exhibits, on the historic communities occupying the ridgeline traversed by the Federal Road. Located on CR-10, near the junction with CR-16 in the Warrior Stand community. Generally open one Saturday per month from 11:00 A.M. to 2:00 P.M. For more information, visit http://www.digtheridge.com.

Creekwood. This Greek revival plantation house, built prior to 1850 and now listed in the National Register of Historic Places, is a private residence viewable only from the public highway. At Creek Stand, just north of the intersection of CR-10 and CR-79, travelers can glimpse Creekwood.

Sand Fort Historic Marker, Seale. The marker incorrectly places construction of this earthwork during the first Creek War. It was likely constructed in the spring of 1836 by General Thomas Jesup. Very little is known about the structure. Following the Creek War, Royston's Inn stood near the abandoned fort. Today a historic marker placed by the Historic Chattahoochee Commission and the Russell County Historical Commission memorializes both places. The marker is located at 5347 CR-22, Seale.

Scott-Yarbrough House, Auburn, Alabama. The historic Scott-Yarbrough House, built in 1847 in the Greek Revival cottage style typical of planter houses of the period, is now a museum known as Pebble Hill. The home is part of the Caroline Marshall Draughon Center for the Arts and Humanities in the College of Liberal Arts at Auburn University. It showcases American antiques and a collection of early Alabama pottery.

Visitors following the Old Federal Road will enjoy the display of early Alabama maps, as well as a collection of McKenney and Hall lithographs of well-known nineteenth-century Creek headmen. Located at 101 Debardeleben Street, Auburn. Tours available on request during normal business hours. Call 334-844-4946 for more information.

Jule Collins Smith Museum of Fine Art. One of the largest art museums in Alabama, the Jule Collins Smith Museum at Auburn University features a variety of original art, including the Advancing American Art collection of over one hundred paintings by mid-twentieth-century American artists and an extensive collection of Belleek pottery from Northern Ireland. Federal Road aficionados will be drawn to one of the museum's core holdings, the Louise Hauss and David Brent Miller Audubon Collection, which contains more than one hundred prints from John James Audubon's *Birds of America* series and other works. Located at 901 South College Street, Auburn University (approximately 3 miles from AL-29/College Street exit 51 off Interstate 85N). Open Tuesday through Saturday 10:00 A.M. to 4:30 P.M. and Sunday 1:00 to 4:00 P.M. There is a café on the premises. For more information, call 334-844-1484.

John James Audubon, *Black Vulture or Carrion Crow*, plate 106, *Birds of America*, 1827–38. Courtesy of the Jule Collins Smith Museum of Fine Art, Auburn University.

*Tuskegee National Forest. Created in 1959 from land that had been clear-cut and severely eroded, Tuskegee National Forest today offers hikers, bikers, and horseback riders opportunities to observe wildlife along the 8.5-mile Bartram Trail, the first in Alabama to receive a National Recreation Trail designation.

Taska Recreation Area, open year-round, includes picnic and sanitary facilities. Primitive camping is allowed seasonally at designated locations. The ranger station is located at 125 National Forest Road 949, Tuskegee. For information about the trail and a trail map, visit www.fs.usda.gov/alabama. For information, call 334-727-2652.

*Tuskegee, which takes its name from a nearby Creek Indian town, was first settled by Americans in the early 1830s and featured several prominent inns for travelers along the Old Federal Road. The area around the town rapidly developed into cotton plantations and many of the enslaved people brought to work the land traveled along the Old Federal Road. Tuskegee Normal School for Colored Teachers, one of the nation's oldest historically black colleges, was established in 1881 and rose to prominence under the leadership of Booker T. Washington and George Washington Carver. Now Tuskegee

University, the institution soon became an epicenter for black education in the south. Throughout the twentieth century, Tuskegee played a pivotal role in the civil rights movement and was the focus of the landmark voting rights case *Gomillion vs Lightfoot*. During World War II, hundreds of black pilots trained in the area. These men, the first African Americans to serve as pilots in the American military, are famously known as the Tuskegee Airmen. The area was also the location of the notorious Tuskegee Syphilis Study. Tuskegee is the birthplace of civil rights era icon Rosa Parks and internationally-known musician Lionel Richie and his R&B group the Commodores. Today, Tuskegee's many museums and historic sites continue to promote the town's prominent role in African American history. Tuskegee History Center, formally the Tuskegee Human and Civil Rights Multicultural Center, tells the story of the town's development from ancient times to the present, with an emphasis on the civil rights movement and the Tuskegee Syphilis Study. The museum is located at 104 South Elm Street. Call for current visitor hours, 334-724-0800. Tuskegee Institute National Historic Site sits a few blocks northwest of the History Center. Visitors can tour buildings on the historic campus, the George Washington Carver Museum, and home of Booker T. Washington. For more information, visit the National Park Service's website, www.nps.gov/tuin.

SECTION TWO

Central Segment

In the central part of the state, much of the Old Federal Road is now abandoned or obscured by later construction. As settlements such as Montgomery and Greenville formed off the original route, numerous branches appeared. Parts of the old road fell into disuse and were incorporated into private property. Once famous tavern stops disappeared long ago, but early settlements and churches along the original course and later branches of the Federal Road testify to its key role in the settlement of Alabama.

Driving Tour: Tuskegee to Mount Meigs

Motorists can follow the Old Federal Road with few deviations through eastern Macon and western Montgomery Counties on existing paved or dirt public roads, although some of the old route is now in private hands. Travelers can access the route at Tuskegee by continuing the driving tour from the eastern segment or by exiting I-85E at Tuskegee/Notasulga (exit 38) onto AL-81 and proceeding to Tuskegee (approximately 3.75 miles). At the intersection with US-80, follow signs to head west. After traveling approximately 9 miles, the road crosses Calebee Creek, near the Creek War battlefield of that name, and joins with the original route of the Old Federal Road. Follow US-80 for another 5 miles. After you pass CR-7, turn left onto a short connector to CR-8/ Old Federal Road. **Cubahatchie Church and Cemetery** is about 1 mile west, on the right side of the road. George Stiggins's historic marker stands at the entrance to the church. One and a half miles beyond the church, CR-8/Old Federal Road merges with US-80. Enjoy the rural scenery as you continue

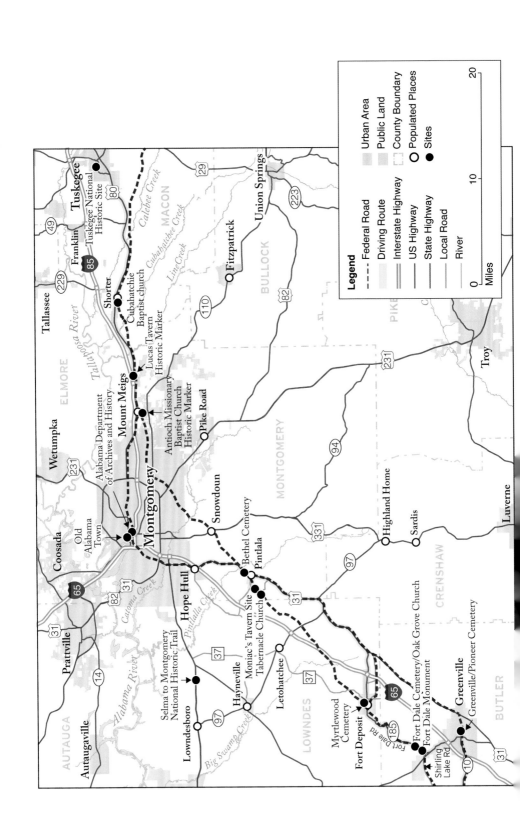

Legend

- - - Federal Road
━━━ Driving Route
━━━ Interstate Highway
━━━ US Highway
━━━ State Highway
━━━ Local Road
━━━ River

Urban Area
Public Land
County Boundary
○ Populated Places
● Sites

0   10   20
Miles

Cubahatchie Baptist Church. Courtesy of Gregory A. Waselkov.

along US-80 for 6 miles to the site of Lucas Tavern, identified by a historic marker on the right side of the road. Continue another 0.7 of a mile to Waugh.

Near Waugh, the original route heads south onto private property and is lost in Montgomery's suburban and urban sprawl. In the 1820s, as Montgomery's population and commercial and political influence increased, a branch road connected the city's thriving waterfront on the Alabama River to the main road. Although the central segment driving tour ends at Waugh, travelers are encouraged to explore the historic sites of Montgomery and continue with the central segment cemetery driving tours.

Driving Tour: Waugh to Shorter/Cubahatchie Baptist Church

Exit I-85 at the Waugh exit and proceed east along US-80 for approximately 0.6 of a mile to the historic marker on the north side of the highway for the original site of Lucas Tavern.

Proceed east 6 miles, then turn right onto CR-8/Old Federal Road. **Cubahatchie Baptist Church** is 1.5 miles on the left.

Archaeological investigations by University of South Alabama archaeologists at the site of Moniac's Tavern, Pintlala, 2011. Courtesy of the Center for Archaeological Studies, University of South Alabama.

Driving Tour: Montgomery to Pintlala

Heading south from Montgomery on I-65, take exit 164 to US-31 toward Pintlala, following a branch of the Old Federal Road. **Bethel Cemetery** is approximately 6 miles from the exit on the left. From Bethel Cemetery, head south on US-31 about 0.75 of a mile to the intersection with CR-24, noting the historic marker for the Old Federal Road. Turn right on CR-24 (Old Federal Road) and proceed just over 1 mile. Turn left on Federal Road, just after crossing Pinchony Creek, noting a second historic marker for the Old Federal Road. The historic site of **Moniac's Tavern**, on private property, is 0.5 of a mile on your left. Continue heading south for approximately 1 mile to **Tabernacle Church** and cemetery. This section, perhaps the most picturesque remaining vestige of the Old Federal Road, continues for about 0.5 of a mile beyond the church to the Lowndes County line. Beyond this point the Old Federal Road is a private dirt road with no public access.

Fort Dale Cemetery, grave houses constructed of cedar and cypress uprights and covered with cedar shakes. Originally erected in the early nineteenth century, the existing grave houses have been extensively restored. Photograph by W. N. Manning, 1935. Courtesy Historic American Buildings Survey, Library of Congress.

Driving Tour: Pintlala to Fort Dale to Greenville

From Pintlala, continue south for 16 miles on US-31S, a route that approximates a branch of the Old Federal Road. Turn right onto AL-185S and proceed 6 miles, past the historic town of **Fort Deposit**, then keep left to remain on AL-185. This scenic byway coincides with the original route of the Old Federal Road. **Oak Grove Church** is approximately 8 miles on the left, and **Fort Dale Cemetery** is 0.5 of a mile farther on the right. Continue on AL-185S for 5.5 miles to **Greenville**. Turn left on Commerce Street. In 0.1 of a mile, turn right on South Park Street. **Pioneer Cemetery** is approximately 0.1 of a mile on your left.

Sites and Places to Visit

__Museum of Alabama, Alabama Department of Archives and History.__ Located on the Montgomery branch of the Old Federal Road, this state-of-the-art museum explores Alabama's history from ancient to modern times. Visitors can explore permanent exhibits that highlight the state's geology and natural resources, native peoples, and social and cultural development. A comprehensive exhibition, *Alabama Voices,* allows visitors to view artifacts, documents, art, and audiovisual presentations detailing Alabama's early history, including the Old Federal Road. Downtown Montgomery, 624 Washington Avenue, directly across from the Alabama State Capitol. Parking is in the rear of the building off Adams Street. The museum is generally open 8:30 A.M. to 4:30 P.M., Monday through Saturday, except on state holidays. For more information, visit http://www.archives.alabama.gov.

*Selma to Montgomery National Historic Trail. The final leg of the famous civil rights march from Selma to Montgomery, in March 1965, largely followed US-31 to the state capitol. Subsequent construction of the I-65/I-85 intersection covered a portion of that route, but other sections survive. The original path of US-31 from Montgomery to Pintlala essentially coincides with the Montgomery branch of the Old Federal Road.

*Old Alabama Town. This historic village comprises rescued structures dating from the nineteenth and early twentieth centuries that otherwise would have been lost to modern development. Begun in 1967 as an effort to save the historic Ordeman House, this outdoor museum is now home to over fifty former residences and businesses laid out over six blocks in downtown Montgomery. Lucas Tavern, built to serve travelers on the Old Federal Road, originally stood just west of Line Creek, which marked the boundary between the Creek Nation and territory ceded to the United States after the Creek War. Walter B. Lucas took over the tavern's operation in 1821; General Lafayette famously visited the establishment four years later. Moved from its original location to Old Alabama Town in 1978, it now serves as Visitor and Information Center for the Old North Hull Historic District. Group and self-guided walking tours of Old Alabama Town are available. Children and seniors receive discounts on the admission fee. The Loeb Reception Center is located at 301 Columbus Street, Montgomery. Open 9:00 A.M. to 4:00 P.M., Monday through Saturday. Admission is charged. For more information, call 334-240-4500.

*Fort Toulouse/Fort Jackson Park. Situated at the confluence of the Coosa and Tallapoosa Rivers, this site has witnessed thousands of years of human occupation, including a Mississippian ceremonial center, a series of French colonial forts, several Creek Indian villages, and the American fortification

Lucas Tavern today, Old Alabama Town. Courtesy of Kathryn Braund.

where the Creek War ended. Early trails led to the site, which was visited by William Bartram. After the Creek War, a branch of the Federal Road took travelers here, where it was presumed an American city would develop, an ambition thwarted by the rise of Montgomery. Today, the park is run by the Alabama Historical Commission and features an RV campground, boat launch, picnic facilities, and a nature trail. In addition to an Indian mound (ca. AD 1100), visitors can explore a small museum, replica French fort, Creek Indian dwellings, and partially restored Fort Jackson. The park is located at 2521 West Fort Toulouse Road, Wetumpka. Admission is charged. For more information, call 334-567-3002.

Lucas Tavern Historic Marker is located 3,000 feet south of the original tavern site, just west of Line Creek in Montgomery County. Originally operated by James Abercrombie, after 1821 Walter B. Lucas's tavern boasted of the best hospitality on the Federal Road. The marker is on the north side of US-80, approximately 0.5 of a mile from exit 16 off I-85.

Cubahatchie Baptist Church. The original church was erected in 1838, two years after the forced removal of the Creek Indians. The area was originally known as "Point Comfort," which was shown on the first map to depict the

Federal Road. Prior to Indian Removal, Cubahatchie Tavern was located near this site.

From this important crossroads, paths (and later roads) branched northwest to Fort Jackson and north to the large Creek town of Tuckabatchee, near modern Tallassee. One of the most famous Creek Americans, George Stiggins, is buried in this cemetery near the tavern site. Stiggins, a brother-in-law of William Weatherford, left a manuscript history of the Creek people that chronicles Alabama's origins from a Native American perspective. A historic marker commemorating Stiggins stands on the church grounds. Very near this site, Captain William Walker managed a more famous tavern at Pole Cat Springs Indian Agency. Walker's wife was the daughter of Big Warrior, Speaker of the Creek National Council. That site is on private property. The church is located at 1060 Old Federal Road, Shorter.

Antioch Missionary Baptist Church Historic Marker, Mount Meigs. The first church in Montgomery County, Antioch Baptist Church, was established 1818. From the beginning, enslaved African Americans were an active part of the congregation, and the church prospered and developed as an African American church. Such churches marked the rise of plantation economies along the Old Federal Road. Located at 738 Gibbs Road in the Pike Road community.

Bethel Cemetery. One of the earliest Baptist burial grounds in Alabama, Bethel Cemetery was founded in 1819. The church built in 1823 was ultimately dismantled. This site, listed on the Alabama Register of Landmarks and Heritage, is now maintained by Pintlala Baptist Church. Numerous Confederate veterans, as well as many early settlers, are buried here. A historic marker at the site explains the difference between Primitive and Missionary Baptists, a division that split the church in the early nineteenth century. The cemetery is on the east side of US-31, 0.75 of a mile north of the CR-24 (Pintlala) intersection.

Tabernacle Church. Erected as a log cabin in 1846 and rebuilt at the end of the nineteenth century, Tabernacle Church is one of the oldest Methodist churches in Montgomery County. Although services are no longer held here, today the structure houses the Tabernacle Historical Association. Church grounds and cemetery are open to visitors, but the church is not open to the public. Located 1.5 miles from the intersection of CR-24 (Federal Road/Cloverfield Road) and Federal Road near Pintlala.

Fort Deposit/Myrtlewood Cemetery. Founded in 1813, Fort Deposit supplied General Claiborne's troops during their march against the Red Stick Creek stronghold of Holy Ground. After the war, some of the earliest Americans to claim ceded Creek lands settled here. Fort Deposit's oldest cemetery, Myrtlewood contains the graves of these founding families. Myrtlewood Cemetery is located on Edgewood Drive in Fort Deposit.

Fort Dale Cemetery/Oak Grove Church. The cemetery dates to 1818 and is named for frontiersman Samuel Dale, who erected a small militia fort near this spot. The cemetery boasts several grave houses dating to the early nineteenth century. Oak Grove Methodist Episcopal Church and the historic site of Fort Dale are less than 0.5 of a mile north of the cemetery. Located at 2410 Fort Dale Road, Greenville.

Greenville/Pioneer Cemetery. Founded in 1819, Greenville was named for its resemblance to the founder's hometown in South Carolina. Underlain with fertile soil suitable for growing cotton, emigrants flocked to the new town. In 1821, the seat of Butler County moved from Fort Dale to Greenville. A branch of the Old Federal Road connected the burgeoning city to the main route. Pioneer Cemetery contains the remains of the city's early settlers, including the county's namesake, Captain William Butler. Several graves are covered with giant cockle shells or cast-iron grave covers, patented by a Greenville native. Located at 216 South Pine Street, Greenville.

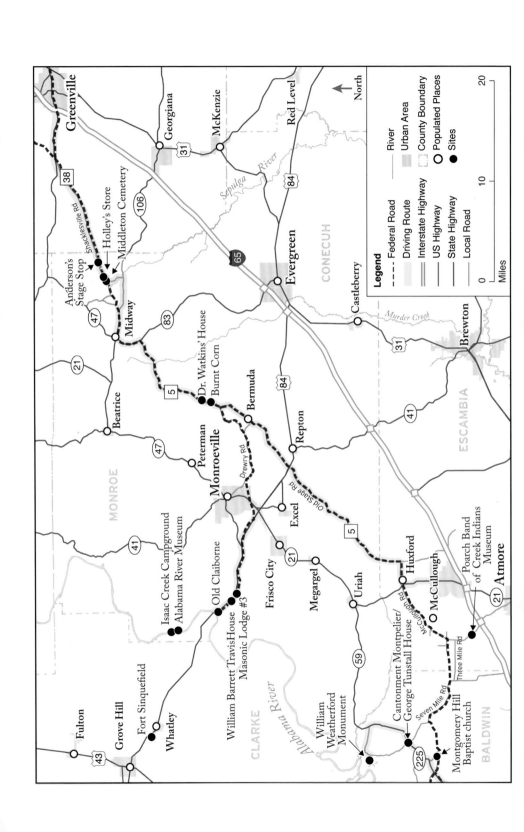

SECTION THREE

Southern Segment

The southern segment of the Old Federal Road is one of the best-documented sections of the road and, like the eastern segment, is closely identified with Creek War events.

Driving Tour: Monroe and Conecuh Counties

The Old Federal Road coincides with most of the Monroe-Conecuh County boundary and generally corresponds to modern paved roads and well-maintained dirt roads. From Atmore, in Escambia County, exit I-65 onto AL-21N (exit 57) toward Uriah and proceed approximately 8 miles to the junction with AL-30/McCullough/Huxford Road. Turn right and head east to Butler Street, which becomes Conecuh CR-45. Turn left. Approximately 1.7 miles north, turn right on Old Stage Road/Conecuh CR-5. This road, a combination of pavement and graded dirt, continues along the approximate path of the Old Federal Road for about 40 miles to the junction with CR-83. Travelers will pass by **Dr. Watkins's House** and through the historic town of **Burnt Corn**. Turn north onto CR-83 toward Midway. Proceed 3 miles and turn right on AL-47N. Continue for 0.1 of a mile and turn right on AL-106E. In 6 miles, turn left onto CR-29. Head north on CR-29 for 2.2 miles. After a hard left curve, turn right on Middleton Road/CR-38, an unmarked dirt road. Proceed along CR-38 for about 4 miles to the Butler County line, passing **Middleton Cemetery**. Most of the historic structures associated with this stretch of road have been lost with time. Travelers can continue to Greenville, in the central portion of the guide book, by following CR-38 for 10.5 miles to the intersection with CR-10. Turn right and proceed 8 miles on CR-10 into Greenville.

A portion of the Old Federal Road in Escambia County. Courtesy of Gregory A. Waselkov.

Sites and Places to Visit (from South to North)

Poarch Band of Creek Indians Museum. Operated by the only federally recognized Indian tribe in Alabama, the museum highlights Creek Indian

Burnt Corn, Alabama. Courtesy of Kathryn Braund.

history and culture. *Kerretv Chuko* (Building of Learning) also serves as the tribe's cultural center, where young Poarch Band members are introduced to Muskogee language and arts. Located at 5811 Jack Springs Road, Atmore, the museum is open Monday through Friday, 8:00 A.M. to 5:00 P.M. For more information, call 251-368-9136.

Burnt Corn. Visitors to this historic hamlet will be very near the locations of James Cornells's stage stop and the intersection with the Wolf Trail to Pensacola. The present town of Burnt Corn was settled after the Creek War. In addition to the picturesque Lowrey's Store, travelers will drive by a number of historic buildings, none currently open to the public. Burnt Corn is located at the crossroads of CR-5 and CR-30.

Dr. Watkins House. Dr. John Watkins, a graduate of the University of Pennsylvania, was virtually the only trained physician in the Mississippi Territory. He first settled in Claiborne, but moved to Burnt Corn in 1819, during the

Dr. John Watkins House, near Burnt Corn, 1934. Watkins was not only one of the earliest doctors in the region but also Alabama's first state judge and a postmaster. Courtesy of the Historic American Buildings Survey, Library of Congress.

Alabama Territorial period. In addition to his medical practice, he was active in early Alabama politics. A historic marker for the house, built circa 1815, is located approximately 1.5 miles north of Burnt Corn on the west side of CR-5. The house is privately owned and not open to the public.

Middleton Cemetery. One of the oldest in the region, this cemetery famously holds the remains of victims of the Stroud "massacre" by Creek Indians in the aftermath of the Creek War. The cemetery is in Monroe County on CR-38, off CR-29.

Driving Tour: Monroeville to Fort Claiborne

An early branch of the Old Federal Road veered west at Burnt Corn toward Fort Claiborne. The old road is largely inaccessible in this location, but the vicinity of the fort site can be reached from Monroeville. There are no

Lafayette at Claiborne, 1825. Cartoon in *Arrow Points* 10 (May 5, 1925): 61, from *Montgomery Advertiser*. Courtesy of Montgomery Advertiser.

standing structures today at the site of the old fort, but travelers can view several buildings formerly of Claiborne at nearby Perdue Hill, including the **Perdue Hill Masonic Lodge** and the **William Barrett Travis House**. Perdue Hill is 13 miles west of Monroeville. Beginning in Monroeville's town square, take West Claiborne Street (AL-47S/W) for 5 miles. Make a slight right onto US-84W and proceed 6 miles to Perdue Hill. From Perdue Hill, continue west approximately 2 miles on US-84 to Claiborne Road. A historic marker noting the approximate location of Fort Claiborne stands just past the intersection of Lena Landegger Highway/Grain Elevator Road, on the south side of the highway.

Proceed along US-84 to the Alabama River bridge to find a historic marker for the townsite of old Claiborne.

Sites and Places to Visit

__William Barrett Travis House.__ This small cottage, built in 1820, was the home of Claiborne lawyer William Travis, who later moved to Texas and shared command at the Alamo, where he died in battle in 1836. His house was relocated from Claiborne to Perdue Hill in 1985. The home is located along US-84 at Perdue Hill.

__Masonic Lodge #3.__ The oldest building in Monroe County, the lodge was built in 1824 at Claiborne. The upper floor served as a masonic hall, while the lower floor saw use as town hall, church, courtroom, and school. General Lafayette spoke at the building in 1824. Located at US-84 and CR-1. Moved to its present location in 1884 and restored in 1981 by the Perdue Hill–Claiborne Foundation, it is open for special events only.

The Masonic Hall at Perdue Hill, 1934. Photograph by W. N. Manning. Courtesy the Historic American Buildings Survey, Library of Congress.

Hayden's Dogs, adapted by Sarah Mattics from *Red Eagle and the Wars with the Creek Indians of Alabama*, by George Cary Eggleston (New York: Dodd, Mead, 1878). At Fort Sinquefield, a man named Hayden mounted his horse and called his dogs to warn the people gathered nearby of an impending Indian attack. Courtesy of the Clarke County Historical Society.

Isaac Creek Campground. The park, which is maintained by the US Army Corp of Engineers, provides river access and a boat ramp as well as campsites, picnic facilities, and birding/hiking trails. It is located at the Claiborne Lock and Dam. From the site of old Claiborne, take Lena Landegger Highway and CR-17/Lock and Dam Road 26 miles to Isaac Creek Road and follow the signs.

Alabama River Museum. In addition to fossils and Indian artifacts, there are exhibits on Alabama River steamboat traffic at this county-owned museum, located on the east bank of the river at Claiborne Lock and Dam at 31 Isaac Creek Road. The museum is open for special events or by appointment only. For more information, visit https://www.monroecountymuseum.org.

Fort Sinquefield. A stockaded blockhouse was built here by early settlers at the outbreak of the Creek War. Although not located on the Federal Road, the inhabitants reached their destination after traveling the road into what was then the Mississippi Territory, on the edge of the Creek Nation. Today, visitors to the park can view a historic marker as well interpretative panels that detail historical events, including the Kimbell-James Massacre. This county park is open to the public during the day. From Claiborne, head west to Whatley on US-84 for approximately 15.5 miles to Fort Sinquefield Road. Take a left to reach the park. Just prior to Sinquefield Road, a historic marker commemorating Kimbell-James Massacre is on the right, at the intersection with Main Street.

Driving Tour: Mobile to Fort Stoddert

Fort Stoddert, located on the west bank of the Mobile River, was the western terminus of the Old Federal Road. From Fort Stoddert, travelers could continue west to the Natchez district, southwest to New Orleans, south to Mobile, or north to St. Stephens, Alabama's territorial capital. For this tour, take US-65N from Mobile to exit 19. Keep left on US-43N for about 30 miles to Mount Vernon. US-43 closely parallels an early branch of the Federal Road.

The Mount Vernon History Trail begins at the intersection of US-43 and Coy Smith Highway/CR-96. A series of eight interpretative panels introduces visitors to Searcy Hospital, Mount Vernon Arsenal, Fort Stoddert, and other places of interest. For more information, visit the Mount Vernon Museum and Train Depot at the junction of State Street and Coy Smith Highway/CR-96.

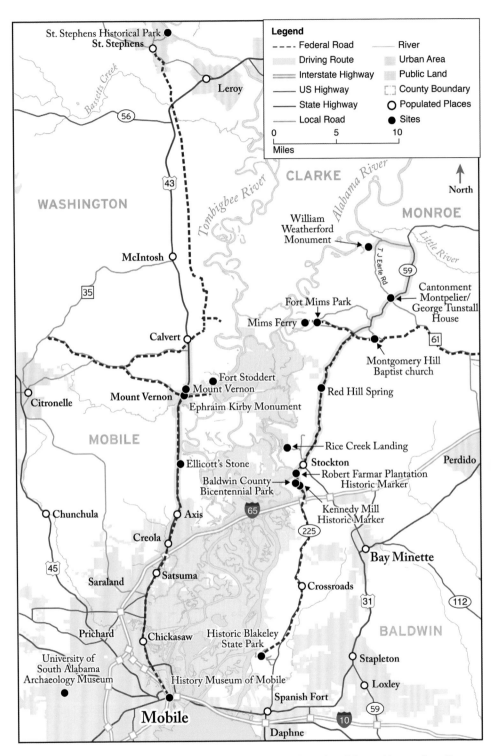

Mobile to Fort Stoddert and Creek War sites along the Old Federal Road in Alabama. Map produced by Brad Sanders.

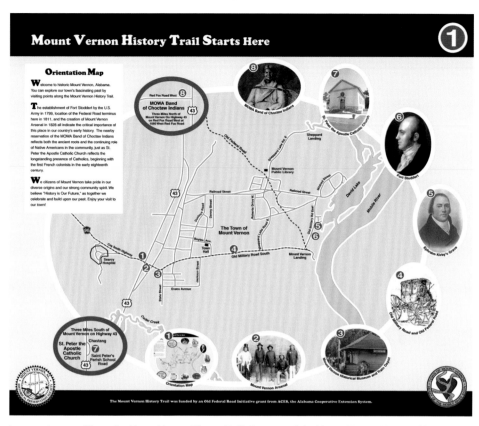

Interpretive panel from the Mount Vernon History Trail. Courtesy of the Mount Vernon Historical Society.

Sites and Places to Visit

History Museum of Mobile. Housed in Mobile's Southern Market and Municipal Building, built in 1855 and now a National Historic Landmark, this museum provides visitors with an excellent overview of Mobile's complex history, from its French colonial origins to the present day. Mobile's seizure by the US Army from Spanish control in the spring of 1813 was one result of the newly built Federal Road. Located at 111 South Royal Street, Mobile, AL, 36602, the museum is open Monday through Saturday, 9:00 A.M. to 5:00 P.M. and on Sunday, 1:00 to 5:00 P.M. There is an admission charge. For more information, call 251-208-7569.

University of South Alabama Archaeology Museum. Exhibits highlight archaeological artifacts excavated from historic sites in the region, including

The site of Fort Stoddert, looking north. Courtesy of Gregory A. Waselkov.

Creek War battlefields and Old St. Stephens, Alabama's territorial capital. Located on the University of South Alabama campus at 6052 USA South Drive, Mobile, AL, 36688, the museum is open Tuesday through Friday, 9:00 A.M. to 4:00 P.M. Admission is free. For more information, call 251-460-6106.

Fort Stoddert. The fort was established in 1799, on a bluff overlooking the Mobile River, to protect US interests along the boundary with Spanish West Florida. Aaron Burr was held briefly at the fort, following his arrest for treason in 1807. The fort became the western terminus of the Federal Road in 1811. Fort Stoddert's historic marker and an interpretive panel are located alongside Old Military Road, north of Mount Vernon Landing. The fort site is on private property.

Mount Vernon Cantonment, Mount Vernon Arsenal, Mount Vernon Barracks, Searcy Hospital. Due to the unhealthy swamps adjacent to Fort Stoddert, most of the garrison relocated 3 miles west in 1811 to Mount Vernon Cantonment, which played an important role in the Creek War. The US Army established Mount Vernon Arsenal on the site in 1828. State militia seized that federal ammunition factory at the outbreak of the Civil War.

Renamed Mount Vernon Barracks, the US Army held Geronimo's band of Chiricahua Apaches here as prisoners of war from 1887 to 1894. Near the end of the nineteenth century, the federal government donated the military reserve to the state of Alabama, which converted the buildings for use as a psychiatric hospital for African American citizens. Finally desegregated in 1969, the state Department of Mental Health still owns Searcy Hospital, although unoccupied since its closure in 2012. While many of the original arsenal buildings are still standing, the site is not open to the public. Historic markers and an interpretative panel can be seen along Superintendents Drive, off Coy Smith Highway/CR-96.

Ephraim Kirby Monument. Erected in memory of Colonel Ephraim Kirby, judge of the first superior court held in what became the state of Alabama, then part of Mississippi Territory. A veteran of the American Revolution, Kirby died at Fort Stoddert in 1804. Kirby's grave in the Fort Stoddert Cemetery is now lost. His monument is on Old Military Road near Old US-43, 2.5 miles west of the Fort Stoddert site.

St. Stephens Historical Park. Now a state park with camping, fishing, boating, and swimming opportunities, the site was once Alabama's territorial capital. The community of San Esteban arose here during the Spanish colonial period. When a formal survey relocated the boundary between the United States and Spanish West Florida miles to the south, the Spanish abandoned their fort and American immigrants soon made St. Stephens a thriving town that rivaled Mobile in size and prosperity. After its heyday in Alabama's territorial period, St. Stephens quickly declined and today is an impressive ghost town with extensive archaeological remains preserved within the park. Located 36 miles north of Mount Vernon via US-43, on the Tombigbee River.

Historic Blakeley State Park. The town of Blakeley was the terminus for a branch of the Federal Road. Today, the park features nature trails on the edge of the Mobile-Tensaw Delta designed for walking, biking, or horseback riding. The park preserves and interprets the site of the largest Civil War battle in Alabama, as well as ancient Indian settlements. From I-65, proceed south on AL-225 for 15 miles; the park is on the right. Park hours are 8:00 A.M. until dusk every day. Located at 34745 State Highway 225, Spanish Fort, AL 36577.

5 Rivers Alabama Delta Resource Center. This educational and recreational complex is located at the junction of the Mobile, Spanish, Tensaw, Apalachee, and Blakeley Rivers at 30945 5 Rivers Boulevard, Spanish Fort, AL 36527. Visitors can learn about the delta area at the exhibit hall and theater, rent canoes or kayaks, and arrange boat tours. There are walking trails and a picnic area and visitors can obtain information on a variety of canoe and kayak trails maintained by the state. The facility is operated by the Alabama Department of Conservation and Natural Resources. Admission is free. The complex is open daily from 8:00 A.M. to 5:00 P.M. For more information, call 251-625-0814.

Meaher State Park. This state park has self-guided walking trails along the Mobile Bay wetlands, a boat ramp and fishing pier, and camp sites. Located across from the 5 Rivers Alabama Delta Center at 5200 Battleship Parkway East, Spanish Fort, AL 36577. The park is open daily from 7:00 A.M. to 7:00 P.M. Call 251-626-5529 for more information. There is a small admission fee for both day use and camping.

Driving Tour: Creek War Sites

In large measure, the Creek War was a direct result of the pressures of American encroachment and settlement brought on by the Federal Road. A cluster of early Federal Road and Creek War sites are located east of the Alabama River in the historic Tensaw settlements that included both American and Creek households. These thriving plantations and communities, which depended on both early travelers and the river for economic prosperity, were engulfed by warfare in the late summer of 1813.

Heading north on I-65, take exit 31 (AL-225N) toward Stockton to view several historic markers and reach Creek War sites.

Sites and Places to Visit

Kennedy Mill. Built in 1811 on an island formed by Rain's Creek, and now located 1.1 miles north of I-65, Joshua Kennedy's sawmill became an early victim of the Creek War. A small detachment of Mississippi Territorial Volunteers commanded by Ensign Isaac Davis, Jefferson Davis's eldest brother, protected civilians who had taken refuge at the mill when Red Stick Creeks destroyed Fort Mims on August 30, 1813. A few days later, Davis led the mill's occupants safely to Mobile. Archaeological remains of the mill were investigated prior to construction of the current bridges. The historic marker commemorating

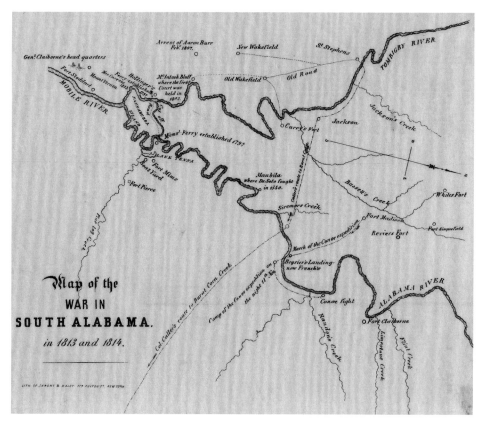

Map of the War in South Alabama in 1813 and 1814, depicting battle sites, forts, and camps, published in 1851. Courtesy of Alabama Department of Archives and History.

the mill is located on AL-225 approximately 1 mile north of I-65, on the right (when traveling north).

Baldwin County Bicentennial Park. A short distance north of Rain's Creek, this park's nature trail highlights the Mobile-Tensaw delta's plants and animals, as well as local history. The park is open Monday through Saturday, 8:00 A.M. to 4:30 P.M. and Sunday noon to 4:30 P.M. Admission is free. For information, call 252-580-1897.

Major Robert Farmar Plantation. The Taensa Indians from Louisiana lived here briefly in the 1720s and gave their name to the district. As commander of the British Thirty-Fourth Regiment of Foot, Major Farmar took possession of

Abandoned section of the Old Federal Road in Baldwin County. Courtesy of Gregory A. Waselkov.

Mobile from the French late in 1763 and soon afterward purchased the Taensa Old Fields. Within ten years he had become the wealthiest planter in the area, with nearly 1,300 acres cultivated by sixty-five enslaved Africans. In 1775 William Bartram used Farmar's plantation, Farm Hall, as a base to explore the region's natural wonders. A historical marker for Farmar's Plantation stands

The large flower evening primrose (*Oenothera grandiflora*) discovered by William Bartram in 1775 near Stockton, Alabama. This late-blooming flower, described by Bartram as "the most pompous and brilliant herbaceous plant yet known to exist," grows in a limited range around Stockton. Courtesy of Kathryn Braund.

on the left side of AL-225, just north of Lower Bryant's Landing Road, 0.75 of a mile north of Bicentennial Park.

Stockton. The town of Stockton arose at the old Farmar plantation site in the mid-nineteenth century but relocated to higher ground to the northeast around 1900. AL-225 ends in Stockton; turn left onto AL-59N. Two historic markers stand on the right along AL-59, which has heavy truck traffic. One marks the Ellicott Line, established by formal survey in 1799 to settle the boundary between Spanish West Florida and the United States. The other commemorates William Bartram's Revolutionary War–era botanical tour of the area.

A local Stockton restaurant continues to recall the importance of stage travel on the Federal Road. Stagecoach Cafe sign, Stockton, Alabama, 2010. Courtesy of the George F. Landegger Collection of Alabama Photographs in Carol M. Highsmith's America, Library of Congress, Prints and Photographs Division.

Rice Creek Landing. Maintained by the Alabama Department of Conservation and Natural Resources (DCNR), this boat ramp offers fishing and recreational access to the Mobile-Tensaw delta for small boats, canoes, and kayaks. After turning onto AL-59N in Stockton, proceed 0.5 of a mile and turn left onto CR-21. Proceed 1.1 miles and turn left onto Rice Creek Road, thence 1.3 miles to the landing. The DCNR maintains the Bartram Canoe Trail, with marked canoe/kayak routes for day trips as well as floating platform campsites. For information on the Rice Creek segment of the Bartram Canoe Trail or for more details about other water trails, call the DCNR at 251-625-0814.

Red Hill Spring. From CR-21, proceed north on AL-59 6.6 miles to Red Hill Spring, an ancient artesian well is still prized locally for the quality of its drinking water.

Montgomery Hill Baptist Church. The modern-day community of Tensaw lies 5.8 miles north of the spring. One of the earliest stage stops on the Federal Road, operated by Mrs. Bryant, was located here when the vicinity was known as Montgomery Hill. The only structure of note remaining today is

Montgomery Hill Baptist Church, built in 1853 and still in use. The Greek Revival–style church, one of two surviving antebellum churches in Baldwin County, is listed on the National Register of Historic Places.

Montgomery Hill Baptist Church lies a short distance east of AL-59. Take either Danny Hall Road or CR-80 east 0.25 of a mile after traveling 5.8 miles north of Red Hill Spring.

Reconstructed blockhouse at Fort Mims. Courtesy of Kathryn Braund.

Fort Mims Park. The Alabama Historical Commission, the Baldwin County Commission, and the Fort Mims Restoration Association jointly manage the 5-acre state park. An annual event in late August commemorates the 1813 Red Stick Creek attack on the fort. The site has picnic tables, reconstructed stockade and blockhouse, monuments, and interpretative panels.

From Montgomery Hill Baptist Church, take CR-80/Boatyard Road west 3.25 miles, then turn right onto Fort Mims Road.

Mims's Ferry. Samuel Mims's old ferry landing is still visible today, immediately south of the mouth of Holley Creek at modern Holley Creek Landing. From this spot on the Alabama River in 1810, Lieutenant Luckett started blazing the Federal Road to the east.

Holley Creek Landing today, the site of the original Mims's ferry crossing of the Alabama River on the Old Federal Road. Courtesy of Gregory A. Waselkov.

From Fort Mims Park, backtrack 0.4 of a mile on CR-80/Boatyard Road and turn left (north) onto Holley Creek Landing Road.
Follow the paved road, bearing left, 1.4 miles to the landing.

Cantonment Montpelier and the George Tunstall House. Following the Creek War, the US Army established a post, just off a new branch of the Federal Road, where a large proportion of the nation's troops were garrisoned until 1821. The site of the cantonment, named for President James Madison's home in Virginia, was built on property belonging to David Tate (one of Alexander McGillivray's nephews and half brother to William Weatherford), famous in his day as a wealthy Creek who opposed the Red Sticks.

From Boatyard Road in Tensaw, turn north onto AL-59 and proceed 5.9 miles to the rural community of Blacksher. The cantonment site is on the right (looking south), in a sharp bend in the road past Turkey Creek. The property is privately owned and not accessible to the public. However, the George Tunstall house, constructed soon after the cantonment's closure, can be seen from the public highway.

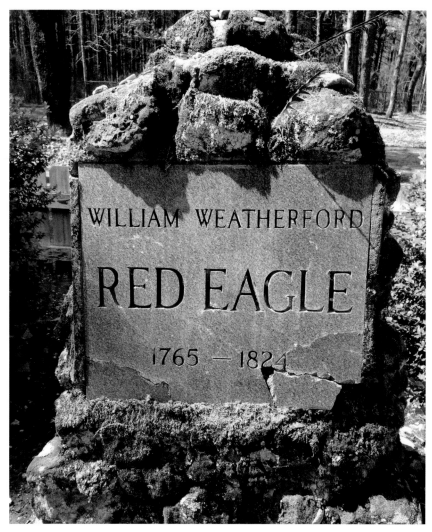

William Weatherford gravesite. Courtesy of Kathryn Braund.

William Weatherford Monument. This small park marks the resting place of William Weatherford, the noted Red Stick Creek warrior, as well as a monument to his mother, Sehoy. From Cantonment Montpelier, proceed northward on AL-59 4.3 miles, past Antebellum Lane on the right, and turn left onto Dixie Landing Road (CR-84). At 2.4 miles, turn left onto T. J. Earle Road and proceed 0.9 of a mile. Red Eagle Road, on the right, leads to the memorial park.

ADDITIONAL RESOURCES

The Old Federal Road website, designed as an accompaniment to this guide, can be found at http://oldfederalroad.info. Please visit the site for additional information, maps, photographs, and links to original travel accounts.

Benton, Jeffrey C. *The Very Worst Road: Travellers' Accounts of Crossing Alabama's Old Creek Indian Territory, 1820–1847.* Tuscaloosa: University of Alabama Press, 2009.

Christopher, Raven M., and Gregory A. Waselkov. *Archaeological Survey of the Old Federal Road in Alabama.* Report prepared for the Alabama Department of Transportation, Project Number STMTE-E09(925). Mobile, AL: Center for Archaeological Studies, University of South Alabama, 2011. https://www.researchgate.net/publication/259398790_Archaeological_Survey_of_the_Old_Federal_Road_in_Alabama_Public_Version_-_Site_Locations_Redacted.

Christopher, Raven, Gregory Waselkov, and Tara Potts. *Archaeological Testing along the Federal Road: Exploring the Site of "Manack's Store," Montgomery County, Alabama.* Mobile, AL: Center for Archaeological Studies, University of South Alabama, 2011. http://www.pintlalahistoricalassociation.com/clientimages/41954/manacks%20store%20report%20-%20final.pdf.

Hudson, Angela Pulley. *Creek Paths and Federal Roads: Indians, Settlers, and Slaves and the Making of the American South.* Chapel Hill: University of North Carolina Press, 2010.

Southerland, Henry deLeon Jr., and Jerry Elijah Brown. *The Federal Road through Georgia, the Creek Nation, and Alabama, 1806–1836.* Rev. ed. Tuscaloosa: University of Alabama Press, 1900.

"The Federal Road Initiative." *Encyclopedia of Alabama.* An online collection of articles devoted to people, places, and events associated with the Old Federal Road. http://www.encyclopediaofalabama.org/federal_road/FederalRoad.jsp.

The Old Federal Road in Alabama: Explore Alabama's History along the Old Federal Highway. An interactive "virtual" Old Federal Road, developed by Terance L. Winemiller, Auburn University, Montgomery. http://oldfederalroad.aum.edu.

NOTES

ACKNOWLEDGMENTS

1. Raven M. Christopher and Gregory A. Waselkov, *Archaeological Survey of the Old Federal Road in Alabama*, report prepared for the Alabama Department of Transportation, project number STMTE-E09(925) (Mobile: Center for Archaeological Studies, University of South Alabama, 2011). A public version of this report can be found online at https://www.research gate.net/publication/259398790_Archaeological_Survey_of_the_Old_Federal_Road_in_ Alabama_Public_Version_-_Site_Locations_Redacted.

2. Raven Christopher, Gregory Waselkov, and Tara Potts, *Archaeological Testing along the Federal Road: Exploring the Site of "Manack's Store," Montgomery County, Alabama* (Mobile: Center for Archaeological Studies, University of South Alabama, 2011). See http://www. pintlalahistoricalassociation.com/clientimages/41954/manacks%20store%20report%20-%20 final.pdf.

PART ONE INTRODUCTION: OPENING THE FEDERAL ROAD

1. Peggy Dow, *The Vicissitudes in the Wilderness: Exemplified in the Journal of Peggy Dow*, 5th ed. (Norwich, CT: William Faulkner, 1833), 55–62. For more information about Dow, see Richard J. Stockham, "The Misunderstood Lorenzo Dow," *Alabama Review* 16 (January 1963): 20–34, and G. Ward Hubbs, "Of Circuit Riders and Camp Meetings, Missionaries and Methodists," *Alabama Heritage* 86 (Fall 2007): 18–25.

CHAPTER ONE: EARLY PATHS AND ROADS

1. K. G. Davies, ed., *Documents of the American Revolution, 1770–1783*, Colonial Office series, 21 vols. (Dublin: Irish University Press, 1972–81), 6:188 (quotation). See Kathryn E. Holland Braund, *Deerskins and Duffels: Creek Indian Trade with Anglo-America, 1685–1815* (Lincoln: University of Nebraska Press, 1993), for information on early trade by deerskin traders.

2. For example, in 1765 the Mortar of Okchai declared to the British, "I am determined that the Path shall not only be made white & streight here but every where." The Mortar at the 1765 Pensacola Congress; Dunbar Rowland, ed., *Mississippi Provincial Archives, English Dominion*, vol. 1 (Jackson: Mississippi Department of Archives and History, 1911), 199.

3. William Bartram, *Travels through North and South Carolina, Georgia, East and West Florida, the Cherokee Country, the Extensive Territories of the Muscogulges, or Creek Confederacy, and the Country of the Choctaws; Containing an Account of the Soil and Natural Productions of Those Regions, Together with Observations on the Manners of the Indians* (Philadelphia: James and Johnson, 1791), 389.

4. Bartram, *Travels*, 396.

5. Bartram, *Travels*, 397.

6. Bartram, *Travels*, 440–42.

7. Bartram, *Travels*, 445.

8. See Kathryn E. Holland Braund, "'Like to Have Made a War among Ourselves': The Creek Indians and the Coming of the War of the Revolution," in *Nexus of Empire: Negotiating Loyalty and Identity in the Revolutionary Borderlands, 1760s–1820s*, ed. Gene Allen Smith and Sylvia L. Hilton (Gainesville: University Press of Florida, 2010), 39–62.

9. C. L. Grant, ed., *Letters, Journals, and Writings of Benjamin Hawkins*, 2 vols. (Savannah, GA: Beehive Press, 1980), 2: 593.

10. Walter Lowrie and Walter S. Franklin, eds., *American State Papers* (hereafter, *ASP*), *Class VII: Post Office Department* (Washington, DC: Gales and Seaton, 1834), 28.

11. *Annals of Congress*, 8th Cong., 1st sess., House of Representatives, November 2, 1803, 555; Henry deLeon Southerland Jr., and Jerry Elijah Brown, *The Federal Road through Georgia, the Creek Nation, and Alabama, 1806–1836* (Tuscaloosa: University of Alabama Press, 1989), 11.

12. H. Thomas Foster II, ed., *The Collected Works of Benjamin Hawkins, 1796–1810* (Tuscaloosa: University of Alabama Press, 2003), 37j–40j.

13. Lowrie and Franklin, *ASP, Class VII: Post Office*, 28. See Briggs-Stabler Papers, MS 147, Mississippi Territorial Survey, Section IIIc, Maryland Historical Society, Baltimore, MD (hereafter MDHS).

14. Clarence Edwin Carter, ed., *The Territorial Papers of the United States*, vol. 5, *The Territory of Mississippi, 1798–1817* (Washington, DC: Government Printing Office, 1937), 306–7.

15. Carter, *Territorial Papers*, 5:306–7; Lowrie and Franklin, *ASP, Class VII: Post Office*, 35–36. Quotes from Briggs to Thomas Jefferson, October 2, 1804, in Briggs-Stabler Papers, MS 147, Mississippi Territorial Survey, Section IIIc, MDHS.

16. Lowrie and Franklin, *ASP, Class VII: Post Office*, 36–38. Quotes from Briggs-Stabler Papers, MS 147, Mississippi Territorial Survey, Section IIIc, MDHS, as follows: Briggs to Thomas Jefferson, October 2, 1804 ("journey," "horses," "red people"); Briggs to Jefferson, November 26, 1804 ("Nathaniel Christmas").

17. Lowrie and Franklin, *ASP, Class VII: Post Office*, 37.

18. Lowrie and Franklin, *ASP, Class VII: Post Office*, 37. Quotes from Briggs-Stabler Papers, MS 147, Mississippi Territorial Survey, Section IIIc, as follows: Briggs to Thomas Jefferson, October 2, 1804 ("About 2 miles"); Briggs to Jefferson, November 26, 1804 ("southeasternmost projection"); September 26, 1804, entry in Survey Notebook ("S.S.W. of the Town").

In his journal, *A Sketch of the Creek Country in the Years 1798 and 1799*, Benjamin Hawkins described the subagency at Point Comfort: "Near one of the bluffs [south of Tuckaubatchee] there is a fine spring, and near it a beautiful elevated situation for a settlement. These hills westwardly are terminated by a small branch and the flat land spreads out for one mile. Below this branch ¼ of a mile is the residence of Oche Haujo (Mr. [Alexander] Cornells), and ½ mile still lower the public establishment; thence two miles to the mouth of Colebehatche. . . . At the public establishment there is a smith's shop, a dwelling house and kitchen built of logs, and a field well fenced. And it is the contemplation of the agent, to have a public garden and nursery." Grant, *Letters, Journals, and Writings of Benjamin Hawkins*, 1:291–92.

19. Additionally, Briggs mentioned staying at the house of Nathaniel Christmas, which he said was two miles above the confluence, so his reference to the mouth of the river seems unambiguous.

20. Thomas Jefferson to A. J. Dallas, February 26, 1816, in Briggs-Stabler Papers, MS 147, Mississippi Territorial Survey, Section IIIc, MDHS. Briggs's field notebook contains several pages of calculations made at the Flint River Agency and at Point Comfort. His nighttime observations of the altitudes of several stars, including Lyra, Pollux, Rigel, α Orionis (Betelgeuse), α Aquila (Altair), Arcturus, and Aldebaran, indicated his chronometer ran around ten minutes slow. For a wonderful modern treatment of the longitude problem, see Dava Sobel, *Longitude* (New York: Walker, 1995).

CHAPTER TWO: BUILDING A FEDERAL ROAD

1. Charles J. Kappler, comp. and ed., *Indian Affairs: Laws and Treaties*, vol. 2, *Treaties* (Washington, DC: Government Printing Office, 1904), 85–86.

2. See Wheaton Papers, No. 4, Rare Book and Manuscript Library, University of Georgia, Athens.

3. See Wheaton Papers, No. 4, Rare Book and Manuscript Library, University of Georgia, Athens.

4. Quoted in Southerland and Brown, *Federal Road*, 29.

5. Grant, *Letters, Journals, and Writings of Benjamin Hawkins*, 2:549.

6. Not in 1803, as surmised by Southerland and Brown, *Federal Road*, 95; See Grant, *Letters, Journals, and Writings of Benjamin Hawkins*, 2:549. Lynn Hastie Thompson, *William Weatherford: His Country and His People* (Bay Minette, AL: Lavender Publishing, 1991), 611.

7. Grant, *Letters, Journals, and Writings of Benjamin Hawkins*, 2:561.

8. Grant, *Letters, Journals, and Writings of Benjamin Hawkins*, 2:568.

9. Minutes of a Survey of the Indian Path or Road East of Alabama leading to or near the Fork or Junction of the Coosa and Tallapoosa, from thence by the Same Path to Highwassee, by Lt. John R. N. Luckett, Baldwin County, Mississippi Territory, September 12th, 1810; Record Group 77, National Archives and Records Administration, Washington, DC. Southerland and Brown, *Federal Road*, 34.

10. Luckett Field Survey Records, Record Group 77, National Archives.

11. Grant, *Letters, Journals, and Writings of Benjamin Hawkins*, 2:570.

12. "From the Georgia Journal," *New-York Herald*, November 24, 1810, 3. Twenty years earlier Samuel Moniac stopped another American intrusion on Creek lands, in the Cumberland River valley, when a war party he led killed all six members of a surveying party. He kept the chief surveyor's compass as a trophy of war. Christina Snyder, "Conquered Enemies, Adopted Kin, and Owned People: The Creek Indians and Their Captives," *Journal of Southern History* 73 (May 2007): 264–65; Braund, *Deerskins and Duffels*, 57.

13. Grant, *Letters, Journals, and Writings of Benjamin Hawkins*, 2:574–75 (quotation), 577–78, 593–94.

14. Grant, *Letters, Journals, and Writings of Benjamin Hawkins*, 2:574–75, 577–78, 581, 590–91, 592–93 (second quotation), 594 (first quotation), 597, 599.

15. *Georgia Journal*, March 25, 1812.

16. Dow, *Vicissitudes*, 59–60.

17. Dow, *Vicissitudes*, 61–62; May Ida Chase, "The Old Federal Road in Alabama" (master's thesis, Birmingham-Southern College, 1936), 51–52.

18. Grant, *Letters, Journals, and Writings of Benjamin Hawkins*, 2:497–98.

19. Grant, *Letters, Journals, and Writings of Benjamin Hawkins*, 2:605.

20. Grant, *Letters, Journals, and Writings of Benjamin Hawkins*, 2:605.

21. Gary Burton, "Pintlala's Cold Murder Case: The Death of Thomas Meredith in 1812," *Alabama Review* 63 (July 2010): 179.

22. Grant, *Letters, Journals, and Writings of Benjamin Hawkins*, 2:606. In this context, "cart" refers to a two-wheeled open vehicle pulled by animal or human, and "chair" refers to a chaise, a covered horse-drawn carriage.

23. H. S. Halbert and T. H. Ball, *The Creek War of 1813 and 1814* (Chicago: Donohue and Henneberry, 1895), 88–89; Grant, *Letters, Journals, and Writings of Benjamin Hawkins*, 2:642–43.

24. Halbert and Ball, *Creek War of 1813 and 1814*, 91–93.

25. Grant, *Letters, Journals, and Writings of Benjamin Hawkins*, 2:643.

26. *An Act for the Relief of Samuel Manac, also, of an Act for the Relief of Certain Creek Indians*, 20th Cong., 1st sess., House Document No. 200 (20-1), Serial Set 173 (Washington, DC: Gales and Seaton, 1828); Raven Christopher, Gregory Waselkov, and Tara Potts, *Archaeological Testing along the Federal Road: Exploring the Site of "Manack's Store," Montgomery County, Alabama* (Mobile: Center for Archaeological Studies, University of South Alabama, 2011).

27. Thomas S. Woodward, *Woodward's Reminiscences of the Creek, or Muscogee Indians, Contained in Letters to Friends in Georgia and Alabama* (Montgomery, AL: Barrett and Wimbish 1859), 93.

CHAPTER THREE: FROM WAR TO STATEHOOD

1. Gregory A. Waselkov, *A Conquering Spirit: Fort Mims and the Redstick War of 1813–1814* (Tuscaloosa: University of Alabama Press, 2006), 159–60, 164–70.

2. Margaret Ervin Austill, "Life of Margaret Ervin Austill," *Alabama Historical Quarterly* 6 (Spring 1944): 98. Freeman's plats can be downloaded from the General Land Office (GLO) website, http://www.glorecords.blm.gov.

3. Karl Davis, "'Much of the Indian Appears': Adaptation and Persistence in a Creek Community, 1783–1854," (PhD diss., University of North Carolina, 2003), 174–75, 187; John T. Ellisor, "'Wild People in the Woods': General Jackson, Savannah Jack, and the First Seminole War in the Alabama Territory," *Alabama Review* 70 (July 2017): 191–221.

4. Clarence Edwin, ed., *The Territorial Papers of the United States*, vol. 18, *The Territory of Alabama, 1817–1819* (Washington, DC: Government Printing Office, 1952), 290–91, 354, 508; Albert J. Pickett Papers, Pickett Family Papers (1779–1904), LPR185, Ia1, Bound Manuscripts, Box 2, "Notes taken from a file of Old Papers in the State Department of Alabama relating to the Indian difficulties in 1818," Interview Notes 11—State Department, and "Notes furnished A. J. Pickett by Mr Reubin Hill of Wetumpka in relation to the killing of Capt Butler and others in Butler County Ala in 1818," Interview Notes, 13—Reubin Hill [1848] (Montgomery: Alabama Department of Archives and History).

5. Adam Hodgson, *Letters from North America Written during a Tour in the United States and Canada*, 2 vols. (London: Hurst, Robinson, 1824), 1:139–40.

6. Francis Paul Prucha, *A Guide to the Military Posts of the United States, 1789–1895* (Madison: State Historical Society of Wisconsin, 1964), 92, 109; Francis Paul Prucha, *Atlas of American Indian Affairs* (Lincoln: University of Nebraska Press, 1990), 96–99, 162; Frank Lawrence Owsley Jr., *Struggle for the Gulf Borderlands: The Creek War and the Battle of New Orleans, 1812–1815* (Gainesville: University Press of Florida, 1981), 112–13; Robert S. Quimby, *The U.S. Army in the War of 1812: An Operational and Command Study* (East Lansing: Michigan State

University Press, 1997), 770, 792; Major Howell Tatum, Topographical Notes and Observations on the Alabama River, August 1814, MSS S-1007, Beinecke Rare Book and Manuscript Library, Yale University; Harold D. Moser, David R. Hoth, Sharon Macpherson, and John H. Reinbold, eds., *The Papers of Andrew Jackson*, vol. 3, *1814–1815* (Knoxville: University of Tennessee Press, 1991), 132–33, 449, 450; Carter, *Territorial Papers of the United States*, vol. 18, *Alabama*, 92–93; William H. Powell, *A History of the Organization and Movements of the Fourth Regiment of Infantry, United States Army* (Washington, DC: M'Gill and Witherow, 1871), 14–16.

7. Albert James Pickett, *History of Alabama, and Incidentally of Georgia and Mississippi, from the Earliest Period*, 2 vols. (Charleston, SC: Walker and James, 1851), 2:379–83; Carter, *Territorial Papers of the United States*, vol. 18, *Alabama*, 290–91; Albert J. Pickett Papers, Pickett Family Papers (1779–1904), LPR185, Ia1, Bound Manuscripts, Box 2, "Notes furnished A. J. Pickett by Mr Reubin Hill of Wetumpka in relation to the killing of Capt Butler and others in Butler County Ala in 1818," Interview Notes, 13—Reubin Hill [1848] (Montgomery: Alabama Department of Archives and History); Moser, Hoth, and Hoemann, *Papers of Andrew Jackson*, vol. 4, *1816–1820*, 30–31, 197–201, 230–31, 239–41; Woodward, *Woodward's Reminiscences*, 83, 91. For the latest study of the region following the Creek War and the repercussions of Creek attacks against settlers, see Ellisor, "Wild People in the Woods," 191–221.

8. Carter, *Territorial Papers of the United States*, vol. 18, *Alabama*, 354–55, 507–9; Carter, *Territorial Papers of the United States*, vol. 5, *Mississippi*, 342, 370.

9. Lowrie and Franklin, *ASP, Class VII: Post Office*, 177–78, 207–8.

10. Walter Lowrie and Walter S. Franklin, eds., *American State Papers, Miscellaneous Documents Legislative and Executive* (Washington, DC: Gales and Seaton, 1834), 466–69.

11. Carter, *Territorial Papers of the United States*, vol. 18, *Alabama*, 178–79, 186–87, 240 (Pickens quote), 374, 415–16, 424–25 (Mitchell quote), 470–71.

12. Harry Toulmin, *A Digest of the Laws of the State of Alabama* (Cahawba, AL: Ginn and Curtis, 1823), 391–92.

CHAPTER FOUR: TRAVELING THE FEDERAL ROAD

1. Harriet Martineau, *Society in America*, 2 vols. (New York: Saunders and Otley, 1837), 1:215.

2. Ella Dzelzainis, *Harriet Martineau: Authorship, Society, and Empire* (Manchester: Manchester University Press, 2011). For Hamilton, see Virginia Brackett, *The Facts on File Companion to the British Novel*, vol. 1, *Beginnings through the 19th Century* (New York: Facts on File, 2006), 493–94. For Royall, see Daniel Walker Howe, *What Hath God Wrought: The Transformation of America, 1815–1848* (New York: Oxford University Press, 2007), 495; Jeffrey C. Benton, ed., *The Very Worst Road: Travellers' Accounts of Crossing Alabama's Old Creek Indian Territory, 1820–1847* (Tuscaloosa: University of Alabama Press, 2009), 57.

3. W. H. G. Armytage, "G. W. Featherstonhaugh, F.R.S., 1780–1866, Anglo-American Scientist," *Notes and Records of the Royal Society of London* 11 (March 1955): 228–35; Edmund Berkeley and Dorothy Smith Berkeley, *George William Featherstonhaugh: The First U.S. Government Geologist* (Tuscaloosa: University of Alabama Press, 1988).

4. Basil Hall, *Travels in North America, in the Years 1827 and 1828*, 2nd ed., 3 vols. (Edinburgh: Cadell, 1830). Margaret Hall's letters to her sister about her tour were published as *The Aristocratic Journey: Being the Outspoken Letters of Mrs. Basil Hall Written during a Fourteenth Months' Sojourn in America 1827–1828*, ed. Dame Una Pope-Hennessey (New York: Putnam's, 1931), 144.

5. Auguste Levasseur, *Lafayette in America in 1824 and 1825*, trans. Alan R. Hoffman (Manchester, NH: Lafayette Press, 2006).

6. Tyrone Power, *Impressions of America during the Years 1833, 1834, and 1835*, 2 vols. (London: Richard Bentley, 1836).

7. "Sol Smith," *Encyclopedia of Alabama*, http://www.encyclopediaofalabama.org/face/Article.jsp?id=h-2423.

8. Phineas Taylor Barnum, *The Life of P. T. Barnum* (New York: Redfield, 1855), and John James Audubon, *Letters of John James Audubon, 1826–1840*, ed. Howard Corning, 2 vols. (Boston: Club of Odd Volumes, 1930; Kraus Reprint, 1969); Mary C. Simms Oliphant, Alfred Taylor Odell, and T. C. Duncan Eaves, eds., *The Letters of William Gilmore Simms*, 5 vols. (Columbia: University of South Carolina Press, 1952).

9. Review of Adam Hodgson's "Remarks during a Journey through North America . . . ," *North American Review*, n.s., 18, no. 43 (April 1824): 221–34.

10. Robert Macfarlane, Stanley Donwood, and Dan Richards, *Holloway* (London: Faber and Faber, 2013).

11. Carl Bernhard, Duke of Saxe-Weimar-Eisenach, *Travels through North America, during the Years 1825 and 1826*, 2 vols. (Philadelphia: Carey, Lea, and Carey, 1828), 2:27 (first quotation) and Tyrone Power, *Impressions of American during the Years 1833, 1834, and 1835*, 2 vols. (Philadelphia: Carey, Lea, and Blanchard, 1836), 2:83 (second quotation).

12. James Silk Buckingham, *The Slave States of America*, 2 vols. (London: Fisher, Son, 1842), 1:250-51; "waxy" quote from G. W. Featherstonhaugh, *Excursion through the Slave States, from Washington on the Potomac to the Frontier of Mexico; with Sketches of Popular Manners and Geological Notices*, 2 vols. (London: John Murray, 1844), 2:317.

13. Thomas Hamilton, *Men and Manners in America* (Edinburgh: William Blackwood, 1833), 2:255.

14. Hodgson, *Letters*, 1:126.

15. Hamilton, *Men and Manners*, 2:255.

16. Bernhard, *Travels*, 2:28.

17. Hamilton, *Men and Manners*, 2:254.

18. James Stuart, *Three Years in North America*, 2 vols. (Edinburgh: Robert Cadell, 1833), 2:167. "Rope dancers" are tightrope walkers. William Gilmore Simms reported that Tuskina stopped the stage in order to mail a letter. Whatever the truth, the incident prompted cries from Americans for federal intervention. With traffic briefly stopped along the road, troops sent to arrest Tuskina failed to find him. Eventually charged with attempting to rob the mail, as well as obstructing its passage, he was cleared of the robbery charge, found guilty of obstruction, and fined. Michael D. Green, *The Politics of Indian Removal: Creek Government and Society in Crisis* (Lincoln: University of Nebraska Press, 1982), 164.

19. Buckingham, *Slave States*, 1:257.

20. Buckingham, *Slave States*, 1:257–58.

21. In 1824, Lukas Vischer reported the usual toll was fifty cents on the Flint River, which was the common charge east of the Chattahoochee. Robert P. Collins, "A Swiss Traveler in the Creek Nation: The Diary of Lukas Vischer, March 1824," *Alabama Review* 59 (October 2006): 257. Bernhard, *Travels*, 2:26.

22. Hodgson, *Letters*, 1:119. "Ninny-pask-ulgees, or Road Indians" was used by Thomas Woodward in his account of the Creek War. Woodward, *Reminiscences*, 37.

23. Hodgson, *Letters*, 1:140.

24. Power, *Impressions*, 2:88.

25. Featherstonhaugh, *Excursion through the Slave States*, 2:316.

26. For example, the ferry at Line Creek was operated by a "hawser stretched across the river." Hamilton, *Men and Manners*, 2:253.

27. Stuart, *Three Years*, 2:165.

28. Hodgson, *Letters*, 1:138–39.

29. Hodgson, *Letters*, 1:123.

30. Hodgson, *Letters*, 1:140.

31. Levasseur, *Lafayette*, 345.

32. John Francis Hamtramck Claiborne, *Life and Times of General Sam Dale, the Mississippi Partisan* (New York: Harper and Brothers, 1860), 173.

33. Hall, *Travels*, 3:285.

34. Hodgson, *Letters*, 1:138–39.

35. For information on stage lines, see Southerland and Brown, *Federal Road*, 60–66.

36. Hodgson, *Letters*, 1:119.

37. Audubon, *Letters*, 2:144.

38. Solomon Franklin Smith, *Theatrical Management in the West and South for Thirty Years* (New York: Harper and Brothers, 1868), 77.

39. Charles Lyell, *A Second Visit to North America*, 2 vols. (London: John Murray, 1855), 2:32.

40. Audubon, *Letters*, 2:114.

41. Hall, *Travels*, 1:93–94.

42. Benton, *Very Worst Road*, 50.

43. Power, *Impressions*, 2:84–85.

44. Power, *Impressions*, 2:72.

45. Power, *Impressions*, 2:73.

CHAPTER FIVE: TAVERNS AND STAGE STOPS

1. Raven M. Christopher and Gregory A. Waselkov, *Archaeological Survey of the Old Federal Road in Alabama*, report prepared for the Alabama Department of Transportation, Project Number STMTE-E09(925) (Mobile: Center for Archaeological Studies, University of South Alabama, 2011), 148–49.

2. Carl McIntire, "Moving West to Mississippi Took Time and Patience in 1819," *Clarion-Ledger* (Jackson, Mississippi), July 20, 1986; Stuart, *Three Years*, 2:210.

3. Basil Hall, *Forty Etchings: From Sketches Made with the Camera Lucida in 1827 and 1828* (Edinburgh: Cadell, 1829), plate 22.

4. For example, see Collins, "Swiss Traveler," 270; Stuart, *Three Years*, 2:191–92.

5. Buckingham, *Slave States*, 1:254–55.

6. Hamilton, *Men and Manners*, 2:262.

7. Hall, *Travels*, 3:285.

8. Stuart, *Three Years*, 2:164.

9. Martineau, *Society*, 1:214.

10. Power, *Impressions*, 2:77.

11. Southerland and Brown, *Federal Road*, 76–77; Christopher and Waselkov, *Archaeological Survey*, 229.

12. Jacob Rhett Motte, *Journey into Wilderness: An Army Surgeon's Account of Life in Camp and Field during the Creek and Seminole Wars*, ed. James F. Sunderman (Gainesville: University of Florida Press, 1953), 19.

13. Joseph G. Smoot, "An Account of Alabama Indian Missions and Presbyterian Churches in 1828 from the Travel Diary of William S. Potts," *Alabama Review* 18 (April 1965): 138–39 (entry for March 22–23). At Sunday services, William S. Potts observed, "The children were all

neat and clean. The boys wear the Indian frocks—the behavior very good, and the lessons well recited. To most of the questions I asked those able to speak English, very sensible answers were returned." There were some thirty pupils at the time of Potts's visit and their families presumably lived nearby, as he encountered "about 30 to 40 adult Indians" at the church service he attended on March 23, 1828. Smoot, "Account of Alabama Indian Missions," 139 (entry for "Sunday 23").

14. Bernhard, *Travels*, 2:26. Bowdoin was a member of the famous Bowdoin family of Massachusetts. Born in England, he came to the United States as a child and graduated from Columbia College. After a stint as a businessman in New York, he returned to England, joined the British army, and served for a time in Egypt. After leaving the army, he briefly returned to America. Nehemiah Cleveland, *History of Bowdoin College: With Biographical Sketches of Its Graduates* (Boston: James Ripley Osgood, 1882), 108. Bowdoin was, according to Bernhard (*Travels*, 2:13), "a very polished man, who had travelled" (2:13). For information on Fort Mitchell, see David W. Chase, *Fort Mitchell: An Archaeological Exploration in Russell County, Alabama* (Moundville: Alabama Archaeological Society, 1974).

15. Anne Royall, *Mrs. Royall's Southern Tour; or, Second Series of the Black Book*, vol. 2 (Washington, DC, 1831), 140–45.

16. Smoot, "Account of Alabama Indian Missions," 137 (entry for March 21, 1828).

17. Stuart, *Three Years in North America*, 2:186, 187.

18. Southerland and Brown, *Federal Road*, 82–83.

19. Hodgson, *Letters*, 1:125.

20. Nella J. Chambers, "Fort Mitchell," *Alabama Historical Quarterly* 21 (1959): 30, 34, 40. She cites a letter from Prince Hughes, the factor, to McKenney, dated January 24, 1820 (M-178-13).

21. Hodgson, *Letters*, 1:123–24; Christopher and Waselkov, *Archaeological Survey*, 229. The Little Prince is often named as a silent partner, but little evidence has been unearthed to substantiate this.

22. Collins, "Swiss Traveler," 268.

23. Edwin C. Bridges, "'The Nation's Guest': The Marquis de Lafayette's Tour of Alabama," *Alabama Heritage* (Fall 2011): 14; Southerland and Brown, *Federal Road*, chapter 5 discusses travelers. Quotation from Levasseur, *Lafayette*, 348 (quotation); Woodward, *Reminiscences*, 72–74, 77.

24. Stuart, *Three Years in North America*, 2:191 (quotation); *American State Papers: Documents, Legislative and Executive, of the Congress of the United States . . . Military Affairs*, 7 vols. (Washington, DC: Gales and Seaton, 1861): 7:332. For information on Sand Fort, see Peter A. Brannon, "Through the Years: Old Sand Fort," *Montgomery Advertiser*, September 2, 1934.

25. Collins, "Swiss Traveler," 269.

26. Southerland and Brown, *Federal Road*, 83.

27. Woodward, *Reminiscences*, 71.

28. Bernhard, *Travels*, 2:28.

29. Margaret Hall in Benton, *Very Worst Road*, 49–50. In 1828, William S. Potts indicated that Lewis's brother also was married to a Creek woman. Both women were "cleanly in their appearance, ornamented with a profusion of beads." Smoot, "Account of Alabama Indian Missions," 141 (entry for Monday 24).

30. Stuart, *Three Years*, 2:191–92. It was later known as Cook's Tavern. William Cowper (1731–1800) was one of the most popular poets of the late eighteenth century. His work dealt with nature and rural life. A convert to evangelical Christianity, he was also the author of popular hymns.

31. Levasseur, *Lafayette*, 348–49.

32. Smoot, "Account of Alabama Indian Missions," 141 (entry for Tuesday 25).

33. Bernhard, *Travels*, 2:29–30.

34. Buckingham, *Slave States*, 1:252–53.

35. Motte, *Journey into Wilderness*, 22.

36. Buckingham, *Slave States*, 1:254–55.

37. Stuart, *Three Years*, 2:203.

38. Buckingham, *Slave States*, 1:260.

39. Hodgson, *Letters*, 1:141–42. The reading was an eclectic mix of modern fiction, poetry, and reference works. *Coelebs in Search of a Wife*, a moralistic novel by Hannah More, was published in 1809; *Camilla: A Picture of Youth*, a wildly popular comedic romance by Frances Burney, appeared in 1796; while Sterne's work was likely *The Life and Opinions of Tristram Shandy* (1759).

40. Christopher and Waselkov, *Archaeological Survey*, 117; see Hodgson, *Letters*, 1:142–43.

41. Clarence Edwin Carter, ed., *The Territorial Papers of the United States*, vol. 6, *The Territory of Mississippi, 1809–1817* (Washington, DC: Government Printing Office, 1952), 673; Carter, ed., *The Territorial Papers of the United States*, vol. 18, *Alabama*, 354–55, 507–9; Lowrie and Franklin, *ASP, Class VII: Post Office*, 135, 177–78, 207–8, 294; Justus Wyman, "Fort Claiborne," *Alabama Historical Quarterly* 19 (Summer 1957): 217; W. Stuart Harris, *Dead Towns of Alabama* (Tuscaloosa: University of Alabama Press, 1977), 71–72.

42. Christopher and Waselkov, *Archaeological Survey*, 134–36.

43. Thomas Stocks, "Memorandum Taken on My Tour to Pensacola Commencing the 15 April, 1819," *Bulletin of the Department of Archives and History* 2 (September 1925): 27.

44. Hodgson, *Letters*, 1:152.

45. Hodgson, *Letters*, 1:118.

46. Hamilton, *Men and Manners*, 2:255, 263.

47. Smoot, "Account of Alabama Indian Missions," 141 (entry for Tuesday 25). Muriel H. Wright, "American Indian Corn Dishes," *Chronicles of Oklahoma* 36 (Summer 1958): 155–66.

48. Hodgson, *Letters*, 1:125.

49. Bernhard, *Travels*, 2:28. This was in 1826.

50. Stuart, *Three Years*, 2:203.

51. Martineau, *Society*, 1:218.

52. Power, *Impressions*, 2:72.

53. Hodgson, *Letters*, 1:125.

CHAPTER SIX: THE CHANGING PHYSICAL AND CULTURAL LANDSCAPE

1. For example, see Power, *Impressions*, 2:88.

2. Hodgson, *Letters*, 1:147–48.

3. Martineau, *Society*, 1:215.

4. Hodgson, *Letters*, 1:147 (frogs); Power, *Impressions*, 2:88 (thunder).

5. Hamilton, *Men and Manners*, 2:254–55.

6. Stuart, *Three Years*, 2:166.

7. Royall, *Mrs. Royall's Southern Tour*, 2:146–47.

8. Martineau, *Society*, 1:215.

9. Martineau, *Society*, 1:216.

10. Hodgson, *Letters*, 1:145–46.

11. Featherstonhaugh, *Excursion*, 2:318.

12. Hodgson, *Letters*, 1:147–49.

13. Lyell, *Second Visit*, 2:34 (rivers), 36 (trees).

14. Lyell, *Second Visit*, 2:36.

15. John R. Swanton, ed., "The Green Corn Dance," *Chronicles of Oklahoma* 10 (June 1932): 178.

16. Hodgson, *Letters*, 1:145.

17. Buckingham, *Slave States*, 1:251.

18. Simms, *Letters*, 1:29. Simms reached the next stage just in time to board.

19. Collins, "Swiss Traveler," 268.

20. Hodgson, *Letters*, 1:117.

21. Levasseur, *Lafayette*, 342.

22. Levasseur, *Lafayette*, 346–37; Hall, *Travels*, 2:289–307; Hamilton, *Men and Manners*, 2:265–68; Hodgson, *Letters*, 1:117.

23. Hodgson, *Letters*, 1:125–26.

24. For example, Hodgson, *Letters*, 1:142–43; Stuart, *Three Years*, 2:167.

25. Bernhard, *Travels*, 2:29.

26. See Smith, *Theatrical Management*, 77–78; Barnum, *Life*, 174–75.

27. Royall, *Mrs. Royall's Southern Tour*, 2:147; Hodgson, *Letters*, 118.

28. Power, *Impressions*, 2:78; Hodgson, *Letters*, 1:117.

29. Power, *Impressions*, 2:78.

30. Hodgson, *Letters*, 1:118–19.

31. Hodgson, *Letters*, 1:119, 126. His tutor was Makittaw. Hodgson recorded some of the names for "articles of dress" in his book.

32. Swanton, "Green Corn Dance," 178–79.

33. Motte, *Journey into Wilderness*, 27–30.

34. Levasseur, *Lafayette*, 343–34.

35. Levasseur, *Lafayette*, 343–44. Hamley was no doubt the son, by a Creek woman, of Colonel William Hambly, the national interpreter for the Creeks.

36. Hodgson, *Letters*, 1:122.

37. Featherstonhaugh, *Excursion*, 2:293.

38. Featherstonhaugh, *Excursion*, 2:314–15.

39. Hall, *Travels*, 3:289.

40. For example, see Levasseur, *Lafayette*, 350–51.

41. Smoot, "Account of Alabama Indian Missions," 141 (entry for Monday 24).

42. Buckingham, *Slave States*, 1:255. He was at a "log-house" between Tuskegee and Cubahatchee.

43. Barnum, *Life*, 174.

44. For information on the Second Creek War, see John T. Ellisor, *The Second Creek War: Interethnic Conflict and Collusion on a Collapsing Frontier* (Lincoln: University of Nebraska Press, 2010). See pp. 193–96 for information on the 1836 attacks on carriages and stages.

45. Mott, *Journey into Wilderness*, 21.

46. "Camp at Tuskegee, July 24" ["Extracts of a letter of an intelligent non-commissioned officer"], *Army and Navy Chronicle*, August 25, 1836, 124.

47. Motte, *Journey into Wilderness*, 20.

48. Audubon, *Letters*, 2:145–46. Brackets inserted by the editor of the published letter have been omitted.

49. Bernhard, *Travels*, 2:31; Hodgson, *Letters*, 1:152 (quotation).

50. Buckingham, *Slave States*, 1:256.

51. Alexander Mackay, *The Western World; or, Travels in the United States in 1846–47*, 2 vols. (Philadelphia: Lea and Blanchard, 1849), 2:265.

52. Martineau, *Society*, 1:216.

53. Christopher D. Haveman, *Rivers of Sand: Creek Indian Emigration, Relocation, and Ethnic Cleansing in the American South* (Lincoln: University of Nebraska Press, 2016) is the most comprehensive study of Creek removal to date.

CONCLUDING REFLECTIONS ON THE FEDERAL ROAD

1. Merriamwebster.com.

INDEX

Page numbers in italics refer to illustrations.